Social Issues
in Literature

War in
Ernest Hemingway's
For Whom the Bell Tolls

Other Books in the Social Issues in Literature Series:

Colonialism in Joseph Conrad's *Heart of Darkness*

Death and Dying in the Poetry of Emily Dickinson

Democracy in the Poetry of Walt Whitman

Depression in Sylvia Plath's *The Bell Jar*

The Environment in Rachel Carson's *Silent Spring*

The Food Industry in Eric Schlosser's *Fast Food Nation*

Poverty in John Steinbeck's *The Pearl*

Race in John Howard Griffin's *Black Like Me*

Race in William Shakespeare's *Othello*

Slavery in Toni Morrison's *Beloved*

Teen Issues in S.E. Hinton's *The Outsiders*

Women's Issues in Zora Neale Hurston's *Their Eyes Were Watching God*

Social Issues
in Literature

War in
Ernest Hemingway's
For Whom the Bell Tolls

Gary Wiener, Book Editor

GREENHAVEN PRESS
A part of Gale, Cengage Learning

Detroit • New York • San Francisco • New Haven, Conn • Waterville, Maine • London

Elizabeth Des Chenes, *Director, Publishing Solutions*

© 2013 Greenhaven Press, a part of Gale, Cengage Learning

Gale and Greenhaven Press are registered trademarks used herein under license.

For more information, contact:
Greenhaven Press
27500 Drake Rd.
Farmington Hills, MI 48331-3535
Or you can visit our Internet site at gale.cengage.com

For product information and technology assistance, contact us at

Gale Customer Support, 1-800-877-4253
For permission to use material from this text or product, submit all requests online at www.cengage.com/permissions

Further permissions questions can be emailed to permissionrequest@cengage.com

Articles in Greenhaven Press anthologies are often edited for length to meet page requirements. In addition, original titles of these works are changed to clearly present the main thesis and to explicitly indicate the author's opinion. Every effort is made to ensure that Greenhaven Press accurately reflects the original intent of the authors. Every effort has been made to trace the owners of copyrighted material.

Cover image © Everett Collection Inc./Alamy.

LIBRARY OF CONGRESS CATALOGING-IN-PUBLICATION DATA

War in Ernest Hemingway's For whom the bell tolls / Gary Wiener, book editor.
p. cm. -- (Social issues in literature)
Includes bibliographical references and index.
ISBN 978-0-7377-6393-5 (hardcover) -- ISBN 978-0-7377-6394-2 (pbk.)
1. Hemingway, Ernest, 1899-1961. For whom the bell tolls. 2. Spain--History--Civil War, 1936-1939--Literature and the war. 3. War in literature. I. Wiener, Gary.
PS3515.E37F7385 2012
813'.52--dc23
2012027205

Printed in Mexico
1 2 3 4 5 6 7 16 15 14 13

Contents

Introduction 9

Chronology 17

Chapter 1: Background on Ernest Hemingway

1. The Life of Ernest Hemingway 23
Gale Contextual Encyclopedia of
American Literature

Ernest Hemingway was one of the great writers and prose stylists of the twentieth century. Early on, as a journalist, he developed the lean prose style that would be a hallmark of his career.

2. Hemingway Learned and Lost from 34
His War Experiences
Peter Moreira

Hemingway's war experiences benefited his fiction but also caused him physical and emotional distress.

3. Writers Tell the Truth About War 47
Ernest Hemingway

A writer's job is to present the truth, but covering a war is a dangerous profession and writers may never live to see the results of their efforts.

4. For Hemingway, War Was Inevitable 52
and Criminal
Erik Nakjavani

Hemingway's pervasive interest in war has left many readers wondering whether he supported violence. Hemingway despised warfare, but, being realistic about its inevitability, he used war to study how people react in extreme situations.

5. Hemingway Kept Politics Out of His Art   **57**
Frederick R. Benson

Hemingway believed that politics was transitory, but art was forever. In writing for posterity, he tried to keep away from politically motivated art.

Chapter 2: *For Whom the Bell Tolls* and War

1. Hemingway Strived to Write About Truth   **63**
Shabnum Iftikhar

Hemingway used his life experience to write *For Whom the Bell Tolls*, showing a realistic portrayal of war.

2. Hemingway Shows All Sides of War   **69**
Peter Messent

In *For Whom the Bell Tolls*, Hemingway uses multiple narrative points of view in order to provide a comprehensive picture of a complex war.

3. Hemingway Refused to Write War Propaganda   **79**
Jeffrey Meyers

While Hemingway and his protagonist in *For Whom the Bell Tolls*, Robert Jordan, both sided against the Fascists during the Spanish Civil War, Hemingway refused to write war propaganda in his novel.

4. Hemingway's Characters Fight for a Cause   **86**
Peter L. Hays

Robert Jordan's stand against Fascism in *For Whom the Bell Tolls* marks a progression for the Hemingway protagonist, who, in Hemingway's earlier works, was wary of causes.

5. *For Whom the Bell Tolls* Is a Novel About How to Die   **96**
Scott Donaldson

During the course of the novel, Robert Jordan receives instruction in how to die. Having learned such a lesson, at the end he rejects suicide and faces his death with dignity.

6. Pilar's Massacre Story Depicts the Brutality   **103**
of Humankind
Allen Josephs

Pilar's massacre story, vividly narrated in great detail, is a
study in humankind's brutality toward other humans. It
was not meant to be a political attack against the Republicans who perpetrated the violence but a statement about
how every death diminishes humankind.

7. *For Whom the Bell Tolls* Is a War Epic   **110**
Carlos Baker

Hemingway's novel takes the form of an epic, similar in
meaning and style to Homer's *Iliad*, as the events at the
Spanish bridge take on universal importance.

8. Maria Is a Victim of War   **116**
Charles J. Nolan Jr.

Critics tend to view Hemingway's women as two-
dimensional. Psychoanalysis of Maria, however, reveals
her to be suffering from post-traumatic stress disorder, a
common aftereffect of war, and her condition creates
empathy in the reader.

Chapter 3: Contemporary Perspectives on War

1. The Afghanistan War Must Be Won   **123**
The Economist

Despite the Afghanistan war's costly toll in lives and dol-
lars, losing the war would exact an even greater toll.
America and Britain must continue their involvement in
Afghanistan until the war is won.

2. The Media Fueled the Run-Up to the Iraq War   **128**
Matthew Rothschild

In the period leading up to the Iraq war, the American
media did not do its job. Instead of casting a critical eye
on the issues, the media let itself be manipulated into
supporting a US invasion.

3. The Spanish Civil War Offers Important   **134**
Lessons About the Iraq War
Stephen Schwartz

The Fascist victory in the Spanish Civil War led to World
War II. An American victory in the Middle East might
just prevent greater conflicts to come.

4. America Failed to Accomplish Its Goals in Iraq   **140**
Jed Babbin

America's attempt to engage in nation building in Iraq
backfired as Islamic militants found ways to subvert US
interests. As the United States pursues its exit strategy, it
is doubtful whether Iraq can become a truly democratic
state.

5. Obama's War Tactics Are Subtle Yet Deadly   **150**
Luiza Ch. Savage

President Obama has shifted his Middle East strategy
away from the large-scale military force that character-
ized the George W. Bush war effort to more precise,
technology-enabled missions. Obama's subtler style of
warfare has proven to be as equally effective as that of
his predecessor.

6. Middle East Revolutions May Not Lead   **157**
to Democracy
Pauline H. Baker

The so-called Arab Spring may lead to the overthrow of
tyrants and dictators, but it does not necessarily ensure
that a democratic state will emerge. The aftermath of
revolution must be carefully orchestrated for a better political system to emerge.

For Further Discussion   **166**

For Further Reading   **167**

Bibliography   **168**

Index   **175**

Introduction

Hemingway loved Spain. He was a world traveler who wrote about many places during his lifetime, but, as critic Allen Josephs says, "no place had the effect on him, as a person or as a writer, that Spain did."[1] When war broke out between the Spanish Republic, supported by the Communist Soviet Union, and the rebels, led by future Spanish dictator Francisco Franco and aided by Adolf Hitler's Nazi Germany and Benito Mussolini's Fascist Italy, Hemingway could not stay away. The Spanish Civil War gave Hemingway the chance to combine two of his great passions: Spanish culture and warfare. War fascinated Hemingway because it gave him the chance to study how human beings behaved in extreme circumstances. In his fiction, he could subject his characters to the crucible of battle and examine what would make them break—or endure. It was no surprise then, that in 1937, Hemingway accepted the North American Newspaper Alliance's offer to report on the Spanish conflict. Critic Matthew J. Bruccoli writes that "Josephine Herbst, who was in Spain with Hemingway, diagnosed the war's pull on him: 'He wanted to be the war writer of his age and he knew it and went toward it.'"[2]

Far into *For Whom the Bell Tolls*, Spanish professor and freedom fighter Robert Jordan remarks that he will write a book about the war once it is over: "He would write a book when he got through with this. But only about the things he knew, truly, and about what he knew." Jordan might as well have been speaking for his creator. Hemingway had written about war and its aftermath before, in short stories, in *The Sun Also Rises*, and in *A Farewell to Arms*, but this novel, which many consider his most ambitious, was to be his magnum opus on the subject, his answer to Leo Tolstoy's monumental *War and Peace*. As Josephs writes, Hemingway's goal was to write a great romantic war novel, his own version of *War and Peace*, a love story between the American volunteer Robert Jordan and the Spanish girl Maria with the real war as background. Hemingway once told the poet Archibald MacLeish that *War and Peace* was the best book he knew. Spain's civil war now provided Hemingway the chance to create his own twentieth-century equivalent of Tolstoy's masterpiece—to create, not simply to report—out of all the raw material of his own experiences in Spain since 1923. He would tell American writer and literary critic Malcolm Cowley some years later that "it wasn't just the civil war I put into it. . . . It was everything I had learned about Spain for eighteen years."[3]

The armed conflict known as the Spanish Civil War was fought during the years 1936–1939. It pitted groups aligned with the left-leaning republic of Spain, known as Loyalists or Republicans, against the rebellious right-wing Fascists, also known as the Nationalists. Up until elections ended the rule of King Alfonso XIII in 1931 (Alfonso was exiled but did not abdicate the throne), Spain had been a monarchy. These elections ushered in the Second Spanish Republic, but it was a tenuous victory. General Francisco Franco, a conservative who fell out of favor once the country moved to the left, amassed an army in Africa and sought to fight his way back into power. But Franco could not cross the Mediterranean Sea, and so he sought help from the Italians and the Germans, both of whom were seeking to expand their fascist reach. They helped air lift Franco's army to southern Spain and provided him with military support for the remainder of the war. Meanwhile, the Spanish Loyalists knew that they would need help to defend their fragile state, so they turned to another country that had overturned its monarchical government, the Soviet Union. That Communist country was only too happy to help defend Spain from the Fascists—for a price. The Spanish government sent the Russians a vast store of gold in exchange for armaments. Along with the weapons came Russian Communist advisers, some of whom were treated quite badly in Hemingway's fictional account of the conflict.

Thus were the opponents set against each other. What began as a failed coup transformed into a long and bitter conflict. The real victims were the Spanish people. Approximately half a million lost their lives and another three hundred thousand fled the country. Hemingway was particularly sensitive to the plight of the common people. His short story "The Old Man at the Bridge," for example, depicts the human cost of the Spanish Civil War. In it, a character very much like Robert Jordan (or Hemingway) meets an old Spanish man who has been forced from his native home of San Carlos. The old man had been taking care of animals in the abandoned town before he was required to leave. "What politics have you?" the Hemingway character asks. "I am without politics," says the old man. "I am seventy-six years old. I have come twelve kilometers now and I think now I can go no further." Hemingway here dramatizes how a man who is involved in nothing more sinister than animal husbandry and who wants no part of the war or affairs of state becomes the true victim of the hostilities.

In addition to troops from Italy, Germany, and the Soviet Union, supporters from other countries, including the United States, streamed into Spain to aid both sides in the conflict. The cosmopolitan nature of the conflict is suggested by the following excerpt from *Mississippi to Madrid* by James Yates, an African American who served in the Abraham Lincoln Brigade, a group of approximately three thousand volunteer soldiers from the United States:

> Small planes continued diving so low that I could see the pilot's faces. When I reached the foxhole I found three men already wedged into the space barely big enough for two. I climbed in on top of them pulling a branch over us. I could hear bullets hitting as they grazed close enough to knock leaves from the branch. One of the men jumped out of the

foxhole and started shouting in perfect English, "Bastards. Fascist bastards!" He turned out to be an Englishman from Liverpool.[4]

Besides the combat troops, a number of famous writers flocked to Spain to serve in, report on, or merely witness the conflict. There was Eric Arthur Blair (pen name, George Orwell) from Great Britain, Pablo Neruda from Chile, André Malraux from France, John Dos Passos from the United States, and, of course, Ernest Hemingway.

With the help of Hitler and Mussolini and the strategic abilities of Franco, the Fascists persevered. They were helped by the disorganization and dysfunction of the Republic. While both sides were composed of a loose collection of groups held together by their hatred for the other side, Franco was able to cement his army together better than his opponents could. Hemingway powerfully dramatizes the dysfunction of the leftists in the scenes where Andrés, Robert Jordan's messenger, tries to warn the Republican officers that their planned attack is doomed, only to be subjected to utter disdain, disregard, and even arrest by superiors such as Lieutenant-Colonel Miranda and André Marty. The war came to a close as military gains by the Fascists destroyed Republican morale. Cities such as Barcelona, Madrid, and Valencia were defeated by or surrendered to the Fascists, and the war ended on April 1, 1939.

Thus *For Whom the Bell Tolls* is the story of a man who endures despite the overwhelming odds against him. Robert Jordan's mission takes on a significance beyond the blowing up of a single bridge in a particular battle. Jordan is a freedom fighter, and his cause is a noble one, even in defeat. Such sentiments represent a major shift in Hemingway's thinking from his earlier novels. Perhaps the most famous passage in Hemingway's *A Farewell to Arms*, which he wrote a decade before *For Whom the Bell Tolls*, was Frederick Henry's expression of the futility of noble causes:

I was always embarrassed by the words sacred, glorious and sacrifice and the expression in vain. We had heard them, sometimes standing in the rain almost out of earshot, so that only the shouted words came through, and had read them, on proclamations that were slapped up by billposters over other proclamations, now for a long time, and I had seen nothing sacred, and the things that were glorious had no glory and the sacrifices were like the stockyards at Chicago if nothing was done with the meat except to bury it.

Ten years later, as the Spanish Civil War presented an opportunity to fight off, however futilely, the march of fascism across Western Europe, Robert Jordan expresses sentiments that are markedly different from those of his predecessor, Henry. By the book's end, Jordan understands that his mission is ill-fated, yet he goes ahead anyway, risking his life, knowing full well he may end up no better than the stockyard meat of which Frederick Henry spoke. As if to drive this home, Hemingway depicts the massacre and decapitation of Loyalist leader El Sordo and his men the day before the climactic scene in which Jordan blows up the bridge. But even in victory, the Fascist leader Lieutenant Berrendo feels no triumph. "What a bad thing war is," he tells himself, shortly after ordering his men to cut off El Sordo's head and wrap it in a poncho.

As Michael K. Solow observes: "A decade earlier, Hemingway had written of desertion and escape from the madness of war—in favor of love—in *A Farewell to Arms* (1929). In *For Whom the Bell Tolls* (1940), the fight against fascism, pitted against love and individuality, emerges as a blunt necessity for which the central character pays the ultimate price."[5] Here Robert Jordan's mission assumes symbolic, universal significance, as the small act of sabotaging a bridge becomes a metaphor for the actions of thousands and millions of freedom fighters. Early in the novel, thinking about the job that he must do, Robert Jordan muses: "There is a bridge and that bridge can be the point on which the future of the human race can turn. As it can turn on everything that happens in this war."

Despite Jordan's heroics, *For Whom the Bell Tolls* is a story about failure. Looking back from a postwar perspective, in 1940 Hemingway would write, "The Spanish civil war was really lost, of course, when the Fascists took [the Basque town of] Iran in the late summer of 1936. But in a war you can never admit, even to yourself, that it is lost. Because when you will admit it is lost you are beaten."[6] In his later novel, *Across the River and into the Trees* (1950), Hemingway's bitterness over the loss in Spain would emerge in protagonist Colonel Richard Cantwell's musings: "If you love a country, you might as well admit it. . . . I have loved three and lost them thrice. Give a credit. We've re-took two [France and Italy]. Retaken, he corrected. And we will retake the other one [from] General Fat Ass Franco."

As the passage suggests, Hemingway unequivocally favored the cause of the Spanish Republic both during and after the war. But as many critics have pointed out, in writing *For Whom the Bell Tolls*, Hemingway abstained from propaganda. He felt that political fiction was myopic. Instead, he chose to present a well-rounded overview of how a cause that was so right went wrong. Along with Fascist atrocities, he depicted a Loyalist massacre of Fascists. The Communist leader André Marty, a real-life figure, draws the heaviest criticism of any character in the novel despite being on the Republican side, while the enemy's Lieutenant Berrendo receives sympathetic treatment. This angered many on the left, who wanted to believe that the world-famous Hemingway was a kindred spirit. But Hemingway was never a doctrinaire politico, and his mission, he believed, was to tell the truth, not what those on the left wanted to hear. As Bruccoli writes, "Hemingway's rejection of political causes and writers who professed them was manifest before the Spanish Civil War. During the early Thirties when leftist orthodoxy was a requirement for literary merit and intellectual respectability, Hemingway sneered at the political converts and conformists. He insisted that political doctrines have nothing to do with enduring literature."[7] In his book *The Battle for Spain* Antony Beevor adds, "The communists did not realize . . . that his deep and genuine hatred of fascism did not mean that he admired them out of any political conviction."[8]

Hemingway did admire the Communists' organizational and fighting capabilities; when it came to the rest of their politics, he was not a believer. Jeffrey Meyers notes that in his war reports, Hemingway emphasized the Loyalist victories and disguised their defeats. But fiction was an altogether different medium. "Released from the obligation to write propaganda," Meyers writes, Hemingway "was now free to criticize the country he loved and the side he had supported, to express his disillusionment with the Spanish character and with the Spanish Left."[9] Hemingway never focused the blame for the Republic's loss on the common people, the ordinary soldiers. He felt that if they had been able to fight on, despite the odds, they might have prevailed. Instead he blamed the politicians and the leaders: He wrote, "The one who being beaten refuses to admit it and fights on the longest wins in all finish fights; unless of course he is killed, starved out, deprived of weapons or betrayed. All of these things happened to the Spanish people. They were killed in vast numbers, starved out, deprived of weapons and betrayed."[10]

In *For Whom the Bell Tolls*, Hemingway attempted to write the war novel for his era, the *War and Peace* of his generation. He may not have wholly succeeded, but sections of the novel come close. Critic Harold Bloom states that "the most memorable episode in *For Whom the Bell Tolls*, El Sordo's last stand with his little knot of partisans against the vastly more numerous and more heavily armed Fascists" is reminiscent of some of Tolstoy's most powerful war fiction. "Hemingway, always Tolstoy's eager student, brilliantly imitates his great original."[11] The novel's staying power is such that sixty-eight years after its publication, during the 2008 Presidential elections, both Republican nominee John McCain and future president Barack Obama listed it among their favorite books. It is no surprise that both men are drawn to Hemingway's quixotic novel. Writing for the *New York Times, Newsweek* editor John Meachem suggests that "like Robert Jordan, they want to make things better and are willing to put themselves in the arena, but they know that nothing is perfectible and that progress is provisional."[12] The essays that follow demonstrate Hemingway's unique ability to dramatize a terrible war in a country that was close to his heart. They depict Hemingway as a truly imaginative artist, one who subordinated his personal beliefs about a war to his greater desire to present all sides of a complicated conflict.

Notes

1. Allen Josephs, "Hemingway's Spanish Sensibility," in *The Cambridge Companion to Ernest Hemingway*, ed. Scott Donaldson. New York: Cambridge University Press, 1996, p. 221.

2. Matthew J. Bruccoli, *On Books and Writers: Selected Essays*, ed. John C. Unrue. Columbia: University of South Carolina Press, 2010, p. 282.

3. Josephs, "Hemingway's Spanish Sensibility, p. 238.

4. James Yates, *From Mississippi to Madrid: Memoir of a Black American in the Abraham Lincoln Brigade*. Seattle: Open Hand, 1989.

5. Michael K. Solow. "A Clash of Certainties, Old and New: *For Whom the Bell Tolls* and the Inner War of Ernest Hemingway," *Hemingway Review*, Fall 2009, p. 104.

6. Ernest Hemingway, Preface to *The Great Crusade* by Gustav Regler. New York: Longmans, Green, 1940, p. vii.

7. Bruccoli, *On Books and Writers*, p. 282.

8. Antony Beevor. *The Battle for Spain: The Spanish Civil War 1936–1939*. New York: Penguin, 1982, p. 246.

9. Jeffrey Meyers, "*For Whom the Bell Tolls* as Contemporary History," in *The Spanish Civil War in Literature*, ed. Janet Pérez and Wendell M. Aycock. Lubbock: Texas Tech University Press, 1990, p. 86.

10. Hemingway, Preface, p. vii.

11. Harold Bloom, *The Western Canon: The Books and School of the Ages*. New York: Harcourt Brace, 1994, p. 336.

12. John Meachem, "How to Read Like a President," *New York Times Sunday Book Review*, November 2, 2008, p. BR27.

Chronology

1899

Ernest Miller Hemingway is born to Clarence and Grace Hemingway on July 21 in Oak Park, Illinois.

1914

World War I begins in Europe.

1917

Hemingway graduates from Oak Park High School and works as a cub reporter for the *Kansas City Star*; the United States enters World War I.

1918

Hemingway serves in the war as an ambulance driver for the American Red Cross; he is wounded on July 8 on the Italian front. The war ends in November.

1920

Hemingway serves as a reporter and foreign correspondent for the *Toronto Daily Star*.

1921

Hemingway marries Hadley Richardson; they move to Paris, France.

1922

Hemingway covers the Greco-Turkish War for the *Toronto Daily Star*.

1923

Hemingway's *Three Stories and Ten Poems* is published by Robert McAlmon in Paris. The Hemingways' son John Hadley (Bumby) is born in October.

1924

A collection of vignettes, *In Our Time*, is published in Paris by Three Mountains Press.

1925

In Our Time, with fourteen short stories added to the original vignettes, is published in New York by Boni & Liveright.

1926

The Torrents of Spring and *The Sun Also Rises* are published by Charles Scribner's Sons.

1927

Hemingway publishes a short-story collection, *Men Without Women*. He marries Pauline Pfeiffer after divorcing Hadley Richardson.

1928

Hemingway moves with Pauline to Key West, Florida, where their son Patrick is born. Clarence Hemingway, the author's father, commits suicide.

1929

A Farewell to Arms is published.

1931

The Hemingways' son Gregory Hancock is born.

1931

Alfonso XIII, king of Spain, flees his country. The Second Spanish Republic is proclaimed. Hemingway buys a home in Key West and lives there for ten years.

1932

Death in the Afternoon is published.

1933

Hemingway publishes a short-story collection, *Winner Take Nothing*.

1934

A Popular Front, composed of leftist and centrist groups, is elected to run Spain.

1935

Green Hills of Africa is published.

1936–1939

The Spanish Civil War is fought as right-wing rebels, led by General Francisco Franco, seek to take control of Spain.

1937

Hemingway travels as a war correspondent to the Spanish Civil War. *To Have and Have Not* is published.

1938

Hemingway collaborates with director Joris Ivens and writer John Dos Passos on *The Spanish Earth*, a film supporting the Loyalist cause in Spain. He publishes *The Fifth Column and the First Forty-Nine Stories*.

1939

Francisco Franco proclaims victory for the Nationalists on April 1. He executes tens of thousands of his Republican enemies as hundreds of thousands of refugees flee Spain.

1939–1945

World War II begins in Europe.

1940

Hemingway divorces Pauline Pfeiffer and marries journalist Martha Gellhorn. He purchases Finca Vigia in Cuba. *For Whom the Bell Tolls* is published.

1941

The Japanese draw the United States into World War II by attacking the US naval base at Pearl Harbor, Hawaii, on December 7.

1942

Hemingway edits the short-story anthology *Men at War.*

1942–1945

Hemingway, as a newspaper and magazine correspondent, covers World War II in Europe and then in China.

1944

Hemingway meets Mary Welsh in London, England. He covers the Allied liberation of Paris, France.

1945

Hemingway divorces Martha Gellhorn.

1946

Hemingway marries Mary Welsh.

1950

Across the River and into the Trees is published.

1951

Grace Hall Hemingway, the writer's mother, dies.

1952

The Old Man and the Sea is published.

1953

Hemingway is awarded the Pulitzer Prize for Fiction for *The Old Man and the Sea.*

1954

Hemingway receives the Nobel Prize for Literature.

1960

Hemingway moves to Ketchum, Idaho. He is hospitalized for uncontrolled high blood pressure, liver disease, diabetes, and depression.

1961

Hemingway commits suicide in Ketchum on July 2.

1964

Hemingway's *A Moveable Feast* is published.

1970

Hemingway's *Islands in the Stream* is published.

1972

Hemingway's *The Nick Adams Stories* is published.

1980

The Hemingway Collection at the John F. Kennedy Library in Boston is opened to the public.

1981

Ernest Hemingway: Selected Letters, edited by Carlos Baker, is published.

1986

The Garden of Eden is published.

1999

True at First Light is published.

Social Issues
in Literature

CHAPTER 1

Background on
Ernest Hemingway

The Life of Ernest Hemingway

Gale Contextual Encyclopedia of American Literature

The Gale Contextual Encyclopedia of American Literature *is a four-volume set that covers American authors from many periods and genres, building a broad understanding of the various contexts—from the biographical to the literary to the historical—in which literature can be viewed.*

Ernest Hemingway was raised in Oak Park, Illinois, a prosperous suburb of Chicago. From an early age, he displayed an interest in writing and journalism, report the authors of the following viewpoint. During his first job as a reporter for the Kansas City Star, *he learned many of the rules for writing that he would employ throughout his career. Hemingway participated in or covered many of the major conflicts of the twentieth century, including World War I, the Spanish Civil War, and World War II. He was awarded the Nobel Prize in Literature in 1954 for his life's work, which included the major novels—*The Sun Also Rises, A Farewell to Arms, For Whom the Bell Tolls—*and the novella* The Old Man and the Sea. *Late in his life Hemingway suffered from depression and insomnia and committed suicide on July 2, 1961.*

Novelist and short story writer Ernest Hemingway was known as much for his masculine behaviors—hunting, fishing, his obsession with the bullfight, his numerous marriages—as for his finely honed prose style, whose spare directness seemed to speak the truth with an unmistakable intensity. Winner of the Nobel Prize in Literature, Hemingway did not just mingle with the literary lights of his generation; his work and his style influenced generations of writers to come.

Early Formative Experience

Hemingway was born in Oak Park, Illinois, an affluent and conservative suburb of Chicago, on July 21, 1899. He was the second of six children and the first son of Clarence Edmunds Hemingway, a physician, and Grace Hall Hemingway. In childhood and adolescence Hemingway spent summers with his family at Windemere, their house at Lake Walloon in northern Michigan. His hunting and fishing adventures and his contact with the Ojibway Indians [aka the Chippewa], as well as his observations of the troubled relationship between his parents, became the material for many of his stories, including "Indian Camp" (1925), "The Doctor and the Doctor's Wife" (1924), and "Fathers and Sons" (1933), all featuring Nick Adams, a recurrent autobiographical protagonist.

The village of Oak Park had a good library and a high school that provided Hemingway with a sound education, especially in composition, language, literature, and history. There he read the great English writers and made his first forays into writing, contributing to the school newspaper and its literary magazine. Hemingway's competitive spirit also drove him to box, play football, and run track, though he was never an outstanding athlete.

Lessons in Journalism

As a student reporter Hemingway was prolific but unexceptional. His experience working for the school paper helped prepare him for his first job, however, as a cub reporter with the *Kansas City Star*, then considered one of the best newspapers in America. In addition to having the advice of first-rate journalistic professionals, Hemingway had to make his writing comply with the one hundred and ten rules of the *Kansas City Star* style sheet, requiring him to avoid adjectives and to use short sentences, brief paragraphs, vigorous English, and fresh phrases. Later, Hemingway remarked that these rules, which influenced his style as a fiction writer, were the best he had ever learned.

World War I had been raging in Europe since 1914, but the United States, which had tried to maintain its neutrality, did not get involved until 1917. Determined to go to Europe and participate in the war effort, Hemingway left the *Kansas City Star* at the end of April 1918 and joined an American Red Cross ambulance unit that assisted the Italian Army, one of America's allies. That July, at Fossalta, he was hit by shrapnel and suffered severe leg wounds; he was sent to an American Red Cross hospital in Milan to recover. His experiences in Italy would later form the basis for his novel *A Farewell to Arms* (1929).

When Hemingway arrived home in January 1919, he attempted a career as a fiction writer, but his work was widely rejected by mass-market magazines. In 1920 he left again, this time for Toronto, to reestablish himself as a journalist by freelancing for the *Toronto Star*. He returned to Chicago in May of that year and worked for *The Cooperative Commonwealth*, a monthly magazine. He met and became engaged to twenty-eight-year-old Hadley Richardson, whom he married in September of 1921. In Chicago he also met Sherwood Anderson, whose *Winesburg, Ohio* (1919) had gained wide acclaim. Anderson befriended Hemingway, encouraged his writing efforts, and convinced him that Paris was the place for a serious writer.

European Horizons

Supported by Hadley Hemingway's trust fund, Hemingway and his wife left for Paris at the end of the year. He carried letters of introduction from Anderson to Sylvia Beach (publisher and owner of the bookstore Shakespeare and Company) and the Modernist writers Gertrude Stein and Ezra Pound. Hemingway met Pound in February of 1922, and the friendship proved to be an invaluable one for Hemingway's development as a writer. Pound helped him hone his style, get his early work published, and also oversaw his literary education, exposing him to the work of [Anglo-American] poet T.S. Eliot and [Irish] novelist James Joyce, whose groundbreaking *Ulysses* (1922) had just been published by Beach. In March of 1922, Hemingway met Gertrude Stein, whose experimental poetry and prose was inspired by the work of the painters with whom she socialized, including Henri Matisse and Pablo Picasso. At her Paris apartment Hemingway studied these artists and especially admired the work of Paul Cézanne; in the original ending to the short story "Big Two-Hearted River" (1925), Hemingway's alter-ego Nick Adams says that he wants to write the way Cézanne painted.

Continuing to work as a stringer for the *Toronto Star*, Hemingway went to Lausanne, Switzerland, in November 1922 to cover a peace conference on a territorial dispute between Greece and Turkey. On the way his wife's suitcase was stolen, and with it Hemingway lost almost all of his unpublished work. The papers were never recovered. In June 1923 Hemingway made his first trip to Spain, where he immersed himself in the culture of bullfighting, which became a perennial favorite subject. He returned again a month later for his first Fiesta of San Fermín in Pamplona, known for its famous running of the bulls.

Becoming Literary

Hemingway's first book, *Three Stories & Ten Poems*, was published in 1923. Although the poems in the volume merited little acclaim, the stories were praised. The Hemingways then left Paris for Toronto, where Hemingway was put on salary as a full-time reporter with the *Toronto Star*. After the birth of their first son, John Hadley Nicanor (Bumby) Hemingway, in October, Hemingway resigned his post and returned to Paris to work on a new journal devoted to experimental fiction, the

Transatlantic Review.

By April 1924 Hemingway's *In Our Time*, a thirty-two-page volume consisting of eighteen vignettes, was on sale in Paris at Shakespeare and Company. It was limited to one hundred and seventy copies and covered themes that would appear repeatedly in Hemingway's later work, including bullfighting and war scenes. Hemingway also began publishing his stories in literary journals (known as "little magazines"). The next year, he signed a contract with Boni & Liveright, a major publisher, to bring out an expanded version of *In Our Time*. Reviewers praised it, but the volume did not sell well. Around the same time, Hemingway met the novelist F. Scott Fitzgerald; their friendship would become one of the most important in Hemingway's life.

In July 1925 Hemingway returned to Pamplona for his second Fiesta of San Fermín with his wife and a diverse group of friends. The excitement of the Fiesta and the tensions among the group formed the basis of Hemingway's first novel, *The Sun Also Rises* (1926), which Hemingway began writing immediately after the adventure ended.

Life's Complications

In 1926 Hemingway and Hadley separated, after it became clear he was involved with Pauline Pfeiffer, a wealthy American who worked for French *Vogue* [magazine]. They divorced in 1927. Soon afterward, Hemingway and Pfeiffer were married. Hemingway had wanted to return to the United States for several years, and he and Pauline, who was pregnant, sailed for Key West [Florida] from France in the spring of 1928. (Their son Patrick was born in June.) In December Hemingway learned, via telegram, that his father had shot himself, having suffered depression for many years. After the funeral, Hemingway finished *A Farewell to Arms* and in the spring brought his family back to France.

Author Ernest Hemingway. © Everett Collection/Alamy.

A Farewell to Arms, published in September 1929, was praised from the outset, and the first printing sold out so quickly as to require three more printings before the end of the year. By February 1930 Hemingway had earned more than $30,000 in royalties. In *The Sun Also Rises* Hemingway had shown the effects of World War I upon the generation whose lives it touched, the so-called "Lost Generation." In his second novel he focused upon the war itself, tracing the events that took a toll on the young people who participated in it.

In November of 1931 Pauline Hemingway gave birth to their son Gregory, and the following month Hemingway finished *Death in the Afternoon* (1932), the novel about bullfighting he had long wanted to write. Although the book revealed Hemingway's considerable research and knowledge about bullfighting, as well as his most extensive public presentation of his writing philosophy, *Death in the Afternoon* was not embraced by Americans.

Hemingway's writing life involved more than just novel writing during this period. He was at work on the story collection that would contain perhaps his most famous story, "A Clean, Well-Lighted Place" (1933), and began contributing articles on hunting and fishing to the brand-new magazine *Esquire*. In 1933 the Hemingways embarked on a two-month African safari, which inspired his next book, *Green Hills of Africa* (1935).

World Events Again Intervene

While work was underway on his next novel, *To Have and Have Not*, Hemingway again heard the call of Spain. The year 1936 saw the beginning of the Spanish Civil War, in which a military uprising led to a three-year-long war between a fascistic military and the left-leaning democratic government of Spain. The efforts of writers like Hemingway and [British writer] George Orwell, who not only traveled to Spain to fight the Fascists but sent home reports on the war, brought international attention to the crisis.

Martha Gellhorn, a young writer whom Hemingway knew in Key West, also went to Spain to report on the war; she and Hemingway soon began an affair. When in 1939 Hemingway moved to Cuba to write his novel about the Spanish Civil War, *For Whom the Bell Tolls* (1940), Gellhorn followed him there, and Pauline filed for divorce. *For Whom the Bell Tolls*, dedicated to Gellhorn, received positive reviews in major American newspapers and in leading magazines. The novel sold 491,000 copies within six months of its publication, and Hemingway's critical reputation, which had declined throughout the 1930s, was once again restored, and his fame and fortune had never been greater. As soon as his divorce from Pauline was final, he and Gellhorn were married at Sun Valley, Idaho, in November of 1940.

After the publication of *For Whom the Bell Tolls*, Hemingway's literary productivity waned. At the end of 1940, at the onset of World War II, he bought the Finca Vigia, his home near Havana, and he and Gellhorn left at the beginning of the new year to cover the war in China—Gellhorn for *Collier's* [magazine] and Hemingway for *PM*, a liberal New York tabloid. In his dispatches for *PM* he often appeared prophetic, predicting correctly that the United States would be forced into war when Japan attacked American bases in the Pacific. He produced just eight articles during his Far East assignment, "only enough," he said, "to keep from being sent home."

With an influx of Nazi agents into Cuba and U-boats [German submarines] steadily sinking ships in the Caribbean, Hemingway proposed to officials at the American Embassy and to the U.S. ambassador to Cuba that he set up a private counterintelligence agency. The Cuban prime minister granted him permission, and Hemingway organized a group he called the Crook Factory, outfitting his fishing boat for U-boat surveillance. During this time Hemingway's drinking increased, and his marriage deteriorated as Gellhorn spent more time away from Cuba on journalistic assignments.

Into the Theater of War

At the end of October 1943 Gellhorn left Cuba again to cover the war in Europe for *Collier's*. Early in 1944 Hemingway usurped her position with the magazine, agreeing to go to Europe for *Collier's* as their front-line correspondent, a role women were not permitted to fill. In this capacity he took part in some of the more iconic moments of the war, the first being the landing of Allied soldiers on Omaha Beach, Normandy, on June 6, 1944, otherwise known as D-Day. Hemingway was posted on a landing craft taking soldiers ashore. He chose to reboard the soldiers' main transport ship rather than try to land with the soldiers, perhaps missing an opportunity but perhaps saving his life: ten other landing craft were destroyed attempting to land. Reporting on the confusion, fear, death, and destruction, Hemingway observed, "Real war is never like paper war, nor do accounts of it read much the way it looks."

Hemingway was also stationed briefly with General George Patton's Third Army and then participated in the liberation of Paris on August 25, 1944. Recalling his feelings about Paris as he looked down on the city with American forces of liberation, he wrote,

> I couldn't say anything more then, because I had a funny choke in my throat and I had to clean my glasses because there now, below us, gray and always beautiful, was spread the city I love best in all the world.

While in Europe Hemingway had begun an affair with Mary Welsh, an American journalist working in London. After the war ended, Hemingway returned to Cuba; Welsh followed him, and after their respective divorces were finalized, they were married, in Havana, in March 1946.

The Last, Erratic Decade

Having published no fiction at all in the 1940s, Hemingway returned to novel-writing, tentatively; the work he produced in the mid-1940s was not published until many years after his death. After a 1948 trip to Italy, Hemingway was finally able to bring a novel to completion; the result was *Across the River and Into the Trees* (1950), which received poor—and at times even hostile—reviews. *The Old Man and the Sea* (1952), which

Hemingway turned to next, proved to be something of a parable of his life in recent years: an old fisherman, having gone eighty-four days without catching a fish, takes his boat far out to sea, spends three days wrestling with an enormous marlin, and then has to battle the sharks to keep his catch. Like the old man, Hemingway suffered a dispiriting dry stretch, but caught his giant marlin with *The Old Man and the Sea*. The story ran in its entirety in five million copies of *Life*, and the 50,000 copies printed in book form sold out in ten days.

The rest of the 1950s brought Hemingway a series of extreme highs and lows. At the end of their 1953–1954 African safari, the Hemingways survived a near-fatal plane crash, only to have their rescue plane crash the very next day. Though they survived the second crash as well, newspapers around the world carried obituaries, many of them riddled with other inaccuracies. Later that year Hemingway was awarded the Nobel Prize in Literature, something which for years he had watched go to writers he believed were undeserving. But, by the end of 1955 Hemingway was laid low again, this time by illness. He bounced back by the end of 1956, well enough to make another trip to Europe and returned to renewed productivity. Back in Cuba, despite his poor health and constant interruptions, Hemingway returned to his work: *True at First Light* (1999), *The Garden of Eden* (1986), and *A Moveable Feast* (1964), a memoir about Paris in the 1920s.

As revolutionary activity increased in Cuba, Hemingway feared he would be a target during the overthrow of the [dictator Fulgencio] Batista government, and he and his wife left Cuba for Ketchum, Idaho. Their move proved to be in the nick of time: [Cuban Communist dictator] Fidel Castro overthrew the government and took control of Cuba on January 1, 1959. The Hemingways departed for Spain in 1959 after Hemingway agreed to write about the bullfight season for *Life* magazine.

During the 1959 Spanish trip—and another in 1960, to gather more material—Hemingway displayed highly erratic behavior. His depression and insomnia growing, his paranoia more obvious, and his nerves uncontrollable, he checked into the Mayo Clinic [medical practice] in Rochester, Minnesota, at the end of November and underwent a series of electroshock therapy treatments. He was released in January of 1961. By March, Hemingway's depression had returned, and he had to be restrained because of suicide attempts. He returned to the Mayo Clinic for additional electroshock therapy in April and was released in June, his psychiatrist confident of Hemingway's improvement. But, back in Idaho, in the early morning of July 2, 1961, Hemingway at last succeeded in killing himself.

Hemingway Learned and Lost from His War Experiences

Peter Moreira

Peter Moreira is the author of Hemingway on the China Front. *He has written for the* Deal, *the* Toronto Globe and Mail, *and the* National Post.

As Moreira writes in the following essay, Ernest Hemingway's life was in many ways defined by the various wars at which he was present. Though he never fought as a soldier, Hemingway served as an ambulance driver or war correspondent in five major conflicts: World War I, the Greco-Turkish War of 1922, the Spanish Civil War, the Second Sino-Japanese War of 1941, and World War II. According to Moreira, war gave Hemingway some of his best stories as well as physical injuries and a severe case of post-traumatic stress disorder. Moreira writes that Hemingway was so drawn to conflict and combat that even in his later years he considered traveling to "attend" the Korean War. Few writers, Moreira says, have used the motif of war as successfully as Hemingway.

Greg Clark didn't believe the war stories told by the American kid who'd wandered into his cluttered Toronto office looking for work. The tall, beefy lad with a limp showed up at the *Star Weekly* [newspaper] in January 1920 and started telling tales about fighting with Italy's famed Arditi commandos in World War I and suffering wounds from mortar explosions and machine-gun fire. The guy must have sensed the features editor's incredulity, for one day he showed up with a small cardboard box. It contained two medals—the *Croce di Guerra* [Cross of War] and *Medaglia d'Argento al Valore Militare* [Silver Medal of Military Valor].

Clark lifted the silver medal, Italy's second highest award for valor, from its box and read the recipient's name etched along its edge: TENENTE ERNESTO HEMINGWAY [Lieutenant Ernest Hemingway].

Manufactured War Stories

The editor, himself a veteran of the 1917 Battle of Vimy Ridge [a battle of World War I fought by the Canadian Corps against the German army], immediately offered young Ernest Hemingway a job. He would later learn, of course, after Hemingway became one of the world's most famous authors, that his suspicions had been well founded. Hemingway had not fought with the Arditi in World War I. He had been a Red Cross ambulance driver, and when he was injured on July 8, 1918, he'd been handing out chocolate and cigarettes to the Italian troops. Yet despite serious wounds he had rescued a wounded soldier and been shot while carrying the man to safety.

Hemingway's 1918 wounding typifies his experiences in war. He visited five battlefronts in his life: the Italian-Austrian front in 1918; the Greco-Turkish War in 1922; the Spanish Civil War in 1937 and 1938; the Second Sino-Japanese War in 1941; and the Allied march through France in 1944. And while anecdotes from each appear in his biography, there is a vagueness about many of them, usually brought on by Hemingway's tall tales about his own exploits. The need to recite manufactured war stories even appeared in his fiction. "His town had heard too many atrocity stories to be thrilled by actualities," Hemingway wrote in "Soldiers Home," a short story about a soldier named Krebs returning to the United States after the war. "Krebs found that to be listened to at all he had to lie."

Sometimes the inaccuracy stems from a tendency by Hemingway's friends, acquaintances or witnesses to exaggerate his feats. These sundry lies and half-truths are pure poison for Hemingway biographers, because often as not the stories are so good the biographer doesn't *want* to doublecheck the facts for fear of losing a real gem. And yet these vague stories are indeed illuminating, because quite often they represent pivotal events in his development as a man and as an artist. Along with bullfighting, hunting, drinking and love, war is one of the enduring motifs of Hemingway's writing and his legendary life.

World War I

World War I was the most important war in Hemingway's development. He had wanted to serve in the Marines or the fledgling Army Air Service but was turned away due to his nearsightedness (in fact, he never served in any of the armed forces). So he joined the American Red Cross ambulance corps in early 1918, when he was not yet 19 years old.

In early June Hemingway arrived in Milan, where he got his first glimpse of war's carnage. He and fellow drivers helped recover the remains of workers killed in a munitions factory explosion. "We found and carried to an improvised mortuary a good number of these," he wrote, "and, I must admit, frankly, the shock it was to find that these dead were women rather than men."

Days later Hemingway was posted to an ambulance unit near Schio, east of Lake Garda, on the border with Austria-Hungary. As well as the practical aspects of the job, there was also a propaganda role—if Italian soldiers saw one American uniform, they might believe others were on their way.

Just after midnight on July 8, Hemingway was dispensing his treats when a round from a muzzle-loaded Austrian trench mortar (described as a five-gallon can filled with explosives and scrap metal) hit near him. "There was a flash, as a blast-furnace door is swung open, and a roar that started white and went red and on and on in a rushing wind," recounts Lieutenant Frederic Henry, Hemingway's semi-autobiographical hero in *A Farewell to Arms*. "I tried to breathe but my breath would not come and I felt myself rush bodily out of myself."

When Hemingway came to, he was buried in dirt. An Italian soldier who'd been between him and the explosion was killed instantly, while another lost both legs. Finding a third, badly wounded soldier nearby, Hemingway hoisted him on his shoulders and, though injured himself, started for an aid station. By some accounts, Austrian spotlights soon tracked the pair, and machine-gun fire caught Hemingway in the right foot and knee. He ran on despite his wounds, covering more than 200 yards to the nearest trench.

The Man and the Image

Contemporary medical accounts recorded 227 shrapnel wounds in Hemingway's legs, though all but about 10 were superficial. While some have questioned the extent of his wounds, the fact remains he had been badly injured and shown remarkable courage. Moreover, this injury may have been the most important episode in his life as an artist. The heroes of his two great novels of the 1920s—Jake Barnes in *The Sun Also Rises* and Frederic Henry in *A Farewell to Arms*— were both injured in World War I, and his short story hero Nick Adams left the war shell-shocked. Philip Young, the most influential Hemingway critic of the 1960s, even put forth a "wound theory," suggesting that the author's life and art comprised repeated attempts to master the primal horror of his wounding at age 18. From this event, Young delineated the Hemingway "code"—the moral imperatives of courage, stoicism and honor by which all Hemingway heroes live.

The injury led directly to the second major event of the war for Hemingway: his love affair with Agnes von Kurowsky. Nine days after the explosion Hemingway was moved to the Ospedale Maggiore, a 16-room hospital in Milan, and promptly fell head over heels for the 26-year-old American nurse. They had a summer romance—unconsummated, she later insisted—that she ended after Hemingway returned to his hometown of Oak Park, Ill., in January 1919. Though their affair was rather brief in the grand scheme of things, its impact on the literary canon was immense; Agnes became the model for Catherine Barkley, Frederic Henry's lover in *A Farewell to Arms*.

World War I shaped Hemingway in many ways. His rapid rise to literary prominence rested in large part on his being a poster boy for the conflict's multitude of physically and emotionally scarred young men—those [expatriate American author] Gertrude Stein called "a lost generation." Most of his great works of the 1920s relied upon and amplified his experiences in the war, and a cornerstone of the Hemingway image was the popular belief he had been wounded in combat in Italy.

The Greco-Turkish War

Hemingway's first brief fling as a war correspondent came in September 1922 while he was living in Paris, when his editors at *The Toronto Star* assigned him to Constantinople to cover the Greco-Turkish War. Infuriating his new wife, Hadley Richardson, who already fretted about his World War I nightmares, Hemingway agreed to cover the conflict shortly after the conquering Turks set fire to the Greek and Armenian quarters in [the Turkish city of] Smyrna.

While in Turkey, Hemingway saw neither combat nor the rumored 260,000 refugees fleeing Smyrna. Only after the armistice was signed on October 11 and Hemingway traveled to Greece did he witness the great migration of refugees from Thrace. He filed vivid accounts to the *Star*, recounting how he marched five miles in the rain with the Thracian peasantry, their possessions strapped to mules and oxcarts. "A husband spreads a blanket over a woman in labor in one of the carts to keep off the driving rain," he wrote. "She is the only person making a sound. Her daughter looks at her in horror and begins to cry."

The Spanish Civil War

It would be almost two decades before Hemingway experienced combat again, and once again the event was associated with a beautiful woman. His coverage of the Spanish Civil War will always be linked to the glamorous war correspondent Martha Gellhorn. Idealistic to a fault and already a published author, Gellhorn was searching for a cause when she met Hemingway in a Key West [Florida] bar, and the erupting conflict in Spain soon became her obsession. Though Hemingway was then married to his devoted second wife, Pauline Pfeiffer, Gellhorn soon became *his* obsession. In no time they agreed to visit the war zone together.

Before leaving, Hemingway signed a contract with the North American Newspaper Alliance (NANA) to report on the conflict—his first real assignment as a war correspondent covering a prolonged conflict. Gellhorn agreed to send dispatches to *Collier's*, then one of America's most popular weekly magazines. He arrived in the spring of 1937, by which time the elected Republican government, backed by the Soviet Union, was besieged in and around Madrid by General Francisco Franco's Nationalist army, allied with Italy and Germany, while battles flared in other parts of the country. Hemingway and Gellhorn reported only what they witnessed, largely because the war was too complicated to describe even in lengthy features. There were at least 40 factions—communists, fascists, anarchists, separatists, unions, youth groups, the Catholic Church—backing one side or the other, and the history of the conflict remains murky, as there were so many versions of each event.

Living in semisecret sin at Madrid's Hotel Florida, Hemingway and Gellhorn reported on the fascist siege of the city and on fighting in [the cities of] Guadalajara and Brihuega. The shelling of Madrid and resulting widespread civilian casualties featured prominently in their writing. "They killed an old woman returning home from market, dropping her in a huddled black heap of clothing, with one leg, suddenly detached, whirling against the wall of an adjoining house," Hemingway wrote in an article that ran on April 11. "They killed three people in another square, who lay like so many torn bundles of old clothing in the dust and rubble when the fragments of the '155' [artillery shell] had burst against the curbing."

Though journalists largely viewed Gellhorn as Hemingway's elegant girlfriend at this point, her articles in *Collier's* soon displayed a gift for restrained and detailed accounts of the suffering war inflicts on common people. Theirs was a rare courtship, an affair intensified by the danger they faced daily, their shared convictions and their association with those celebrities (like [American] writers Virginia Cowles and John Dos Passos) who also roomed at the Florida. And Hemingway, as always, was good company in the war zone—jovial, courageous, ready to share his always-filled hip flask with comrades. The grand hotel itself lay within range of Nationalist shells, charging a dollar a day for rooms up front but considerably more for those facing away from the bombardment.

For the next two years, Hemingway divided his time between Spain, where he recorded the destruction of the Second Spanish Republic, and the United States, where he watched his marriage to Pauline endure a similar fate. In all, he logged three tours of Spain during the war—March to May and September to December 1937, and April to May 1938. During his second sojourn, the Republicans lost [northern Spanish municipality] Bilbao and the Basque areas [in northwestern Spain] and were divided by internal skirmishes. On his third and final journey, the Republicans were retreating to the Mediterranean near Barcelona, and once again Hemingway was reporting on the flight of refugees.

The front had stabilized by the time Hemingway and Gellhorn left Spain, but it was obvious the Republicans had lost. Yet the war brought about a flowering of work by Hemingway. In addition to his NANA articles, he wrote the play *The Fifth Column* and narrated Dutch filmmaker Joris Ivens' propaganda film *The Spanish Earth*, which they screened at the White House in July 1937. And in 1940 the Spanish conflict was the subject of his longest novel, *For Whom the Bell Tolls*, which critic and biographer Jeffrey Meyers calls "the greatest political novel in American literature."

The War Between China and Japan

After marrying Hemingway in late 1940, Gellhorn, who had covered the growing crisis in Europe, wanted to cover the Second Sino-Japanese War. Hemingway reluctantly agreed. Their three-month journey was a disappointment: Gellhorn was sick and hated China, and they witnessed no battles, only a mock operation on the dormant front north of Canton. Hemingway was reporting for the New York daily *PM* [a leftist newspaper], as well as providing intelligence to Treasury Secretary Henry Morgenthau Jr. The writer sent Morgenthau a six-page, single-spaced brief on the complicated situation in China, proving himself a deft gatherer and interpreter of political and military data.

His experience in China apparently gave Hemingway a taste for espionage, for when he returned to his home in Cuba, he organized a network of amateur spies who gathered information for the FBI on Axis [Germany, Italy and Japan] sympathizers and operatives on the island. After this venture fizzled, Hemingway and his drinking buddies used his fishing boat *Pilar* to hunt for U-boats [German submarines], operat-

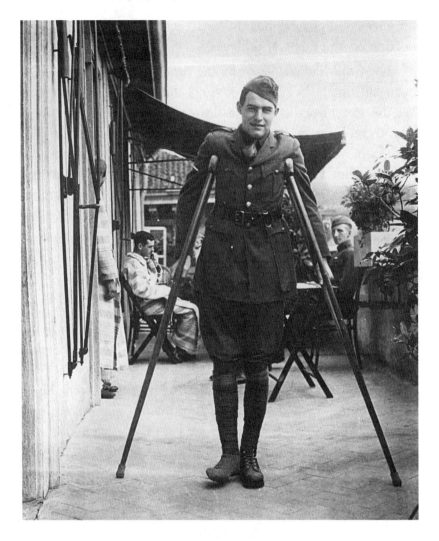

Ernest Hemingway on crutches, circa 1918. He was an ambulance driver for the American Red Cross during World War I and was injured in the line of duty. © Corbis.

ing in the Caribbean, thinking they could surprise one and drop explosives down its conning-tower hatch.

Hemingway also applied to the new [US intelligence agency] Office of Strategic Services (OSS) in 1944. But it turned him down, believing—correctly—he was "too much of an individualist to work under military supervision."

World War II

From 1941 to 1944 Gellhorn covered the war in Europe for *Collier's* from London. Upon returning to Cuba in March 1944, she pleaded with Hemingway to come to Europe. He finally agreed to cover the war, also for *Collier's*. Hemingway received the magazine's front-line accreditation, and as the military allotted only one per publication, he effectively ensured Gellhorn would not receive it (as a woman, she was unlikely to get it at the time anyway). He also arranged a flight to London for himself, leaving Gellhorn to cross the North Atlantic aboard a munitions ship.

By the time Gellhorn arrived in England in late May 1944, Hemingway was enraptured with *Time/Life* magazine correspondent Mary Welsh. The following months were marked by his disintegrating relationship with Gellhorn, his blossoming affair with Welsh, and his legendary contribution to the capture of France and Western Germany.

World War II had less impact on Hemingway's art than his earlier conflicts, as he wrote about the war peripherally only in the mediocre novel *Across the River and Into the Trees* and in stories published posthumously. But his actions in 1944 greatly amplified the Hemingway mystique. In the presence of soldiers and male journalists (who dutifully recorded his exploits), he was a swashbuckling irregular—jolly, courageous, foolhardy. And while he later claimed to have beaten Free French General Philippe Leclerc into Paris and to have liberated the city's famed Ritz Hotel, it is extremely difficult to pin down the facts, as Hemingway—and others—again greatly exaggerated his exploits.

We do know that Hemingway's last war began on the morning of June 6, when he clambered from a troopship into a Higgins boat [landing craft used to ferry platoons in World War II] bound for Normandy's Omaha Beach. Due to confusion on the beach, his craft had to bob off the French coast until the troops could be put ashore. Correspondents were not yet permitted ashore, so Hemingway returned to England aboard a transport and was outraged when he learned Gellhorn had stowed away on a hospital ship and snuck ashore before him.

Hemingway returned to France on July 18 and soon joined the Allied advance on Paris. He considered journalism a poor outlet for his talents and filed only six pieces to *Collier's* from Europe. Hemingway could read maps, speak French and some German, and had an appreciation for tactics. He also possessed a forceful personality and was a natural leader. Hemingway kept in contact with both the OSS and French Resistance and was reportedly armed and shooting at the enemy. On July 30 he "liberated" a German motorcycle with sidecar. Hemingway and his jeep driver, Private Red Pelkey, also flushed six German soldiers from a farmhouse with hand grenades and took them prisoner. Two days later, near Saint-Pois, he spent an afternoon pinned in a ditch by machine-gun fire after a German shell upended his motorcycle. Though his role in the liberation of Paris was frequently distorted, he did arrive in the city on August 25, the day Leclerc's Free French took the city, and Hemingway and his entourage did indeed dine at the Ritz that night.

He continued to travel with journalists (many of whom considered him a reckless braggart) and attached himself to the U.S. 22nd Infantry Regiment, whose commander, Col. Charles "Buck" Lanhara, became a fast friend. Hemingway traveled with the regiment (returning to Paris occasionally to be with Mary Welsh) right through to the bloody fighting in Germany's Hürtgen Forest in the winter of 1944–1945. At one point, the inspector general of the Third Army, prompted by complaints from other correspondents, investigated whether Hemingway's actions in combat violated regulations governing civilian war correspondents. In response, he denied participating in combat.

Cheating Death

Hemingway often displayed an almost insane disdain for danger. On one occasion, he and other guests were dining at Lanham's command post in a farmhouse near the Siegfried Line when a shell crashed through a wall. The others dove into a potato cellar, then peeked out to find Hemingway still at the table, calmly eating his steak. When Lanham ordered him to take cover, the writer replied that a shell would be as likely to hit one place as another, so he would remain where he was. Lanham argued with him as another round came through the wall. The others stayed in the shelter, watching their colonel berate Hemingway as more shells hit.

It's a great story, but it highlights a darker side of Hemingway's behavior. Throughout his time with the 22nd Infantry, Hemingway wrote Welsh letters saying he'd once again cheated the "old whore, Death." Biographer Michael Reynolds concluded that Hemingway—his third marriage a failure and his head still ringing from a concussion sustained in a traffic accident just after his arrival in London—"simply no longer cared if he lived or died."

The fierce combat in the Hürtgen only intensified Hemingway's inner gloom. The 22nd Infantry sustained more than 2,800 casualties in the battle, and the writer was almost among them. Lanham later reported seeing Hemingway armed with a rifle and shooting as the regiment advanced near the infamous "Valley of Death."

On Dec. 3, 1944, Hemingway, Pelkey and *Time/Life* correspondent Bill Walton were riding down an exposed road when Hemingway ordered Pelkey to stop the jeep. They heard a faint hum, then Hemingway yelled, "Oh, God, jump!" The trio landed in the dirt just as a diving German fighter strafed their vehicle. Hemingway had recognized the engine noise from the Spanish Civil War.

Postwar Trauma

Ernest Hemingway did not see combat again after late 1944. He once mentioned to Mary, who became his fourth wife, that he might "attend" the Korean War, but nothing ever came of it The "old whore, Death" never caught up with Hemingway in a war zone, but that's not to say he escaped war unscathed. He suffered nightmares and insomnia for decades after his wounding in Italy, symptoms representative of what is now known as post-traumatic stress disorder.

But while Hemingway suffered from his exposure to war, it inarguably enriched both his life and the body of global literature. Few writers have employed war as a motif so successfully. "After his wounding in World War I, Hemingway viewed armed combat as the most central experience of his century," Reynolds wrote. "Here a man could see his species stripped down to a primal level; here he could test his own emotional resources." Hemingway's own emotional resources were vast, but in the end, they were not infinite.

Writers Tell the Truth About War

Ernest Hemingway

Ernest Hemingway was a world-renowned author and Nobel Laureate. His novels include The Sun Also Rises, A Farewell to Arms, For Whom the Bell Tolls, *and* The Old Man and the Sea.

In this speech to the American Writers' Congress in 1937, Hemingway gives his candid appraisal of the Spanish Civil War. He states that Fascism is a lie and can never produce art, which is about getting at the truth. Those who cover combat, Hemingway suggests, may get used to war, but they never get used to cold-blooded murder. He accuses the Fascists of murdering civilians when they lose battles against other armies. Writers who cover wars such as the Spanish Civil War, Hemingway concludes, engage in a risky profession. They should not worry about whether they will be rewarded for their efforts, as they may die before they ever know whether their reporting has paid off.

A writer's problem does not change. He himself changes, but his problem remains the same. It is always how to write truly and, having found what is true, to project it in such a way that it becomes a part of the experience of the person who reads it.

Fascism Is the Enemy of Writers

There is nothing more difficult to do, and because of the difficulty, the rewards, whether they come early or late, are usually very great. If the rewards come early, the writer is often

Ernest Hemingway, "Fascism Is a Lie," speech to the American Writers' Congress, June 4, 1937. Rpt. in *Conversations with Ernest Hemingway*, ed. Matthew J. Bruccoli. Jackson and London: University Press of Mississippi, 1966, pp. 193–95. Copyright © the University of South Carolina Press. All rights reserved. Reproduced by permission.

ruined by them. If they come too late, he is probably embittered. Sometimes they only come after he is dead, and then they cannot bother him. But because of the difficulty of making true, lasting writing, a really good writer is always sure of eventual recognition. Only romantics think that there are such things as unknown masters.

Really good writers are always rewarded under almost any existing system of government that they can tolerate. There is only one form of government that cannot produce good writers, and that system is fascism. For fascism is a lie told by bullies. A writer who will not lie cannot live or work under fascism.

Because fascism is a lie, it is condemned to literary sterility. And when it is past, it will have no history except the bloody history of murder that is well known and that a few of us have seen with our own eyes in the last few months.

Writers Grow Accustomed to War

A writer, when he knows what it is about and how it is done, grows accustomed to war. That is a serious truth which you discover. It is a shock to discover how truly used to it you become. When you are at the front each day and see trench warfare, open warfare, attacks, and counter-attacks, it all makes sense no matter what the cost in dead and wounded—when you know what the men are fighting for and that they are fighting intelligently. When men fight for the freedom of their country against a foreign invasion, and when these men are your friends—some new friends and some of long standing—and you know how they were attacked and how they fought, at first almost unarmed, you learn, watching them live and fight and die, that there are worse things than war. Cowardice is worse, treachery is worse, and simple selfishness is worse.

In Madrid [Spain], where it costs every British newspaper £57 [British Sterling] or say $280 a week to insure a correspondent's life, and where the American correspondents work at an average wage of $65 a week uninsured, we of the working press watched murder done last month [May 1937] for nineteen days. It was done by German artillery, and it was highly efficient murder.

I said you grow accustomed to war. If you are interested enough in the science of it—and it is a great science—and in the problem of human conduct under danger, you can become so encompassed in it that it seems a nasty sort of egotism even to consider one's own fate. But no one becomes accustomed to murder. And murder on a large scale we saw every day for nineteen days during the last bombardments of Madrid.

Fascist Bullies

The totalitarian fascist states believe in the totalitarian war. That, put simply, means that whenever they are beaten by armed forces they take their revenge on unarmed civilians. In [the Spanish Civil War], since the middle of November [1936], they have been beaten at the Parque del Oeste, they have been beaten at the Pardo, they have been beaten at Carabanchel, they have been beaten on the Jarama, they have been beaten at Brihuega, and at Cordoba, and they are being fought to a standstill at Bilbao. Every time they are beaten in the field, they salvage that strange thing they call their honor by murdering civilians.

You have seen this murder in Joris Ivens's film [*Spanish Earth*], so I will not describe it. If I described it, it would only make you vomit. It might make you hate. But we do not want hate. We want a reasoned understanding of the criminality of fascism and how it should be opposed. We must realize that these murders are the gestures of a bully, the great bully of fascism. There is only one way to quell a bully, and that is to thrash him; and the bully of fascism is being beaten now in Spain as Napoleon [Bonaparte] was beaten in that same peninsula a hundred and thirty years ago. The fascist countries know it and are desperate. Italy knows her troops will not fight outside of Italy, nor, in spite of marvelous material, are they the equal of soldiers of the new Spanish regiments. There is no question of them ever equaling the fighters of the international brigades.

Germany has found that she cannot depend on Italy as an ally in any sort of offensive war. I have read that [German fascist leader Werner] von Blomberg witnessed an impressive series of maneuvers yesterday with Badoglio [Italian fascist leader Marshal Pietro], but it is one thing to maneuver on the Venetian plain with no enemy present, and another to be outmaneuvered and have three divisions destroyed on the plateau between Brihuega and Trijueja [in central Spain], by the Eleventh and Twelfth International Brigades and the fine Spanish troops of [military leaders Enrique] Lister, "Campesino," [name given to Valentin González] and [Cipriano] Mera. It is one thing to bombard Almeria and take an undefended Málaga given up by treachery, and another to lose seven thousand troops before Cordoba and thirty thousand in unsuccessful assaults on Madrid. It is one thing to destroy Guernica and another to fail to take Bilbao [all Spanish Civil War battle sites].

Writing Is a Dangerous Profession

I have talked too long. I started to speak of the difficulty of trying to write well and truly, and of the inevitable reward to those who achieve it. But in a time of war—and we are now in a time of war, whether we like it or not—the rewards are all suspended. It is very dangerous to write the truth in war, and the truth is also very dangerous to come by. I do not know just which American writers have gone out to seek it. I know many men of the Lincoln Battalion. But they are not writers. They are letter writers. Many British writers have gone. Many German writers have gone. Many French, and Dutch writers have gone; and when a man goes to seek the truth in war he may find death instead. But if twelve go and only two come back, the truth they bring will be the truth, and not the garbled hearsay that we pass as history. Whether the truth is worth some risk to come by, the writers must decide themselves. Certainly it is more comfortable to spend their time disputing learnedly on points of doctrine. And there will always be new schisms and new fallings-off and marvelous exotic doctrines and romantic lost leaders, for those who do not want to work at what they profess to believe in, but only to discuss and to maintain positions—skillfully chosen positions with no risk involved in holding them, positions to be held by the typewriter and consolidated with the fountain pen. But there is now, and there will be from now on for a long time, war for any writer to go to who wants to study it. It looks as though we are in for many years of undeclared wars. There are many ways that writers can go to them. Afterward there may be rewards. But that need not bother the writer's conscience. Because the rewards will not come for a long time. And he must not worry about them too much. Because if he is like [British novelist] Ralph Fox and some others he will not be there to receive them.

For Hemingway, War Was Inevitable and Criminal

Erik Nakjavani

Erik Nakjavani is an emeritus professor of humanities at the University of Pittsburgh. He has published essays on American literature, interdisciplinary studies, literary theory, and psychoanalytic criticism. He specializes in Hemingway studies, with an emphasis on psychoanalysis.

Many of Ernest Hemingway's readers questioned why he was so drawn to writing about war. They wondered cynically if he advocated warfare. But Nakjavani makes it clear in the following selection, citing Hemingway's essays on the subject, that the writer considered war a great evil. Nevertheless, Nakjavani argues, Hemingway felt the need to write about war because it was so pervasive in both modern and historical Europe. Hemingway wrote about war to instruct and warn his readers about the criminality of those leaders who wage wars and to admire the bravery and heroism of the combatants. Because Hemingway accepted the inevitability of war, Nakjavani suggests, he was able to use warfare as a vehicle to understand how people operated in life and death situations.

No catalogue of horrors ever kept men from war.—Ernest Hemingway, *By-Line: Ernest Hemingway*

We know war is bad. Yet sometimes it is necessary to fight. But still war is bad and any man who says it is not is a liar.— Ernest Hemingway, *Selected Letters*

Erik Nakjavani, "Hemingway on War and Peace," *North Dakota Quarterly*, vol. 68, nos. 2–3, Spring–Summer 2001, pp. 245–73. Rpt. in *Twentieth-Century Literary Criticism*, ed. Thomas J. Schoenberg and Lawrence J. Trudeau. Vol 162. Detroit: Gale, 2005.

Preoccupied with War

Hemingway's 1949 preface to the illustrated edition of *A Farewell to Arms* (1929) gives him the opportunity to express his views on the topic of war as a persistent dimension of the human condition. "The title of this book is *A Farewell to Arms*," he writes, "and except for three years there has been war of some kind almost ever since it has been written." Considering the enormity of the subject, Hemingway's tone is relatively disillusioned, reticent, and almost detached, without heat or hope, but authoritative. He makes a simple statement that may be boiled down to stating that the lived history of our time is experiential proof of the inevitability of war. He only intimates that the title refers to his World War I (1914–1918) novel, a war of unprecedented mechanized violence and brutality, which was naively hailed by some as the war to end all wars. The intervening years, before and after the publication of *A Farewell to Arms*, were to belie that claim. Wars and other conflicts betrayed even the most modest measure of hope the title in one of its multiple significations might have implied—both on the planes of the individual and the particular and the national and the universal. The three years of uneasy peace to which Hemingway refers could have only been the gift of the total European war weariness and exhaustion, not at all a reassuring reason for the absence of war. After this minimal and highly compressed but essential account of two decades of European history, he then gently makes fun of the critics who irked him by regarding his interest in war as obsessive, even pathological. "Some people used to say," he chides, "why is the man so preoccupied and obsessed with war, and now, since 1933 perhaps it is clear why a writer should be interested in the constant bullying, murderous, slovenly crime of war."

Thus, writing in 1949, for Hemingway nearly the whole first half of the 20th century stands accused of the "murderous, slovenly crime of war," going all the way back to the European 1908–1914 arms race, which he characteristically leaves out. What he does include is the mere mention of the virulent form of the "constant bullying" and the quasi-mystical glorification of murderous impulses in the 1933 rise of Nazi ideology. It is an ideology that regards violence as sacred within the putative prerogatives of the Aryan "master race." Hemingway might have added other bloody events he knew so much about, mainly the 1917 Bolshevik Revolution in Russia, as an armed struggle for a classless society that was to sweep away what Karl Marx and Friedrich Engels in *The Communist Manifesto* decried as "All fixed and fast-frozen [human] relations, with their train of ancient and venerable prejudices and opinions" the surge of Italian Fascism (1922) as the resurgence of the Roman Empire; and the Spanish Civil War (1936–1939). The bipolarity of these two ideologies, Communism and Fascism, found their common ground in totalitarian attitudes, but the Nazi and Fascist ideologies appeared more inclined to acclaim unbound violence as a value in itself. Violence appeared to them to yield a panacea to individual and national powerlessness. In 1935, in his essay "Notes on the Next War," Hemingway warns:

> In a modern war there is no Victory. The allies won the war but the regiments that marched in triumph were not the men who fought the war. The men who fought the war were dead. More than seven million of them were dead and it is the murder of over seven million more that an ex-corporal in the German army [Adolf Hitler] and an ex-aviator and former morphine addict [Benito Mussolini] drunk with personal and military ambition and fogged in a blood-stained murk of misty patriotism look forward hysterically to today.

No Advocate for War

Hemingway's interest as a writer in all the blood-lust and bloodletting in the 20th century is also augmented by the omnipresence of their analogues throughout human history. He reminds us that "Europe has always fought, the intervals of peace are only Armistices." For him, the historical background is a melancholy reminder of our foreground, a gloomy story elaborately and intricately foretold. It is the continual preparation for and perpetual occurrence of war that force Hemingway to consider war as a subject of primary interest for a writer. Persuaded that the foretold are at least forewarned, he sounds an alarm. War, as an atavistic [reverting to an older trait] concern, fascinates him and compels him to reflect. He would have agreed with the Chinese warrior-philosopher Sun Tzu [author of *The Art of War*] who holds that "Military action is . . . the ground of death and life, the path of survival and destruction, so it is important to examine it."

However, I find no reason to suggest that war and its metaphors and metonymies [a form of figurative language] heard as echoes in Hemingway's writing are in any way an advocacy of war. It is tempting to establish a connection between intellectual, literary, and personal interests and advocacy in his case, but I believe it will prove to be wading in the shallows and ultimately a spurious undertaking. It will be so regardless of the occasions for bravery and nobility, which Hemingway greatly admired, that war provides for men. There is too much evidence to the contrary. In his introduction to [the 1946 essay collection] *Treasury for the Free World*, he is unmistakably direct about the criminality of war:

> An aggressive war is the great crime against everything good in the world. A defensive war, which must necessarily turn to aggressive at the earliest moment, is the necessary great counter-crime. But never think that war, no matter how necessary, nor how justified, is not a crime.

In his essay "Wings over Africa," he instructs us that "war has the essence of all of these [tyranny, injustice, murder, brutality, and the corruption of the soul] blended together and is strengthened by its various parts until it is stronger than any of the evils it is composed of can ever be." Thus he does not condone war as admissible or excusable—even though often war may be defensive, unavoidable, and inevitable. For him, as we have just seen, war always conjugates all manifestations of evil in such a way as to make them more effective in their combined demonic violence.

An Unsurpassable Experience

"War is always wrong," [German psychiatrist and philosopher] Karl Jaspers categorically proclaims—plain and simple. No casuistry of just war for Jaspers. It would seem to me Hemingway would have no quarrel with such a straightforward ethical statement. Yet, from a writer's point of view, he considers war to be a significant experience. The experience of war is consequential to him even if a writer peripherally participates in it, as Hemingway did by serving with the Red Cross on the Italian front where he was gravely wounded on July 8, 1918. Accordingly, his understanding of war—as being at once unavoidable and unacceptable, even when it places itself under the sign of counter-violence—deepens and becomes exceedingly nuanced. His fictional references to matters of war testify to the scope and complexity of his comprehension of the subject, even though his own direct war experience was limited. As an exigent life-and-death experience—veritable *extremis* or "limit-situation," as Jasper calls it—war is no doubt for many an unsurpassable and often epiphanic experience.

Hemingway Kept Politics Out of His Art

Frederick R. Benson

Frederick R. Benson taught comparative literature at the City University of New York.

According to Benson in the following excerpts, Hemingway struggled mightily with politics during the Spanish Civil War. Although Hemingway himself claimed in a letter that he always sided with the Republic against the Fascists, he tried to keep politics out of his work. Hemingway felt that art was forever, Benson states, and that politics was transitory: in a thousand years, no one would care about twentieth-century European political controversies. But the Spanish Civil War forced Hemingway the man to side with the Loyalists. He loved Spain and wanted to preserve the country to which he felt so emotionally attached, Benson suggests.

Ernest Hemingway may be termed the most apolitical of the group [of authors writing about the Spanish Civil War]. The Spanish peasant in [Hemingway's story] "The Old Man at the Bridge," who worried about his birds and his cats, said, "I have no politics." From his wound at Fossalta del Piave [in Italy] in World War I to his residence in Madrid's Hotel Florida [during the Spanish Civil War], Hemingway was almost belligerently nonpolitical. He set down his convictions on the relationship between the writer and politics in the fall of 1934, well before the Spanish conflict:

A writer can make himself a nice career while he is alive by espousing a political cause, working for it, making a profes-

Frederick R Benson, *Writers in Arms: The Literary Impact of the Spanish Civil War.* New York: New York University Press, 1967, pp. 60–63. Copyright © 1967 by New York University Press. All rights reserved. Reproduced by permission.

sion of believing in it, and if it wins he will be very well placed. . . . A man can be a Fascist or Communist and if his outfit gets in he can get to be an ambassador, or have a million copies of his books printed by the Government, or any of the other rewards the boys dream about. . . . But none of this will help him as a writer unless he finds something new to add to human knowledge while he is writing.

Hemingway Rejected Political Art

Hemingway rejected political themes, which he felt were transitory in their relevance, and even in the 1930s, when politics and economics were the chief concerns of the intellectuals in America and Europe, he wrote that "a thousand years makes economics silly and a work of art endures forever, but it is very difficult to do and now it is not fashionable." Such a belief does not imply that Hemingway divorced himself from politics during this period. It merely illustrates his feeling that there was a distinct separation between the artist and the man, and this separation must be maintained or great literature will be sacrificed for histories, economic treatises, political expositions, and interpretations of current social trends.

[Hemingway scholar and biographer] Carlos Baker emphasizes that Hemingway's views on man in society were determined, in the 1930s, by three major considerations: his experiences during World War I, in which he saw the violence of modern warfare at first hand; his increasing disgust with and hatred of the postwar machinations of European diplomats and dictators in their struggle for power, which he had covered as a newspaper correspondent; and his ingrained belief that the novelist who pontificated on the course of contemporary history would always tend to betray his true artistic purposes. This third factor in the development of Hemingway's views on the writer in politics was most important. To substitute political propaganda for literature seemed to Hemingway an evasion of the serious writer's fundamental obligation to his art, which was

to write straight honest prose on human beings. First you
have to know the subject; then you have to know how to
write. Both take a lifetime to learn, and anyone is cheating
who takes politics as a way out. It is too easy. All the outs
are too easy, and the thing itself is too hard to do.

The Utopian world envisioned by the political ideologies
of the 1930s did not tempt Hemingway. Perhaps his experience as a foreign correspondent, intimately in touch with political actualities, had released him from such temptation. As
early as the 1920s, Hemingway had been on record as antifascist, but such sentiments were not manifest in his novels of
the period. In his short story, "Che Ti Dice La Patria," [What
Do You Hear from Home?] which appeared in 1927, he left
no doubt about his contempt for [Italian dictator Benito]
Mussolini and Il Duce's [Mussolini's nickname, "The Leader"]
political philosophy. Nor, as Baker notes, was Hemingway an
avid supporter of [Russian Communist leaders Vladimir] Lenin, [Leon] Trotsky, or [Joseph] Stalin, although it is more
difficult to find literary evidence of his displeasure with the
communists than with his violent antifascist sentiments. As a
badly wounded veteran of a war which was the outgrowth of
conflicting political philosophies, Hemingway was bitter about
any talk of "great causes." Throughout the 1920s and early
1930s, he recognized the signs of decadence in European society and the implications inherent in such political decay. But
in his novels of the period he refused to confuse his writing
career with the work of a political commentator.

Reacting to the Conflict

When the economic collapse in Europe and the United States
reinforced the contention of socially-conscious literary critics
on the relationship between literature and social crises and the
necessity for the writer's involvement in the political conflicts
of his time, Hemingway's novels appeared an incongruity. His
literary themes were in another sphere, remote from politics

and everyday affairs, in which was found a preoccupation with violence and an impatience with conventional virtues. "It is difficult to imagine," wrote Wyndham Lewis in 1934, "a writer whose mind is more entirely closed to politics than is Hemingway's." Hemingway's cult of the virile and dynamic virtues, his books on bull-fighting and big game hunting in Africa during the depression years, seemed only to reinforce Lewis' criticism. Before Hemingway's social conscience could be sufficiently stimulated to manifest itself in his novels, a threat to something as personal as his feelings toward Spain and the Spanish people was necessary.

At the second American Writers' Congress in 1937, one radical critic envisioned the transformation of Hemingway from a nonpolitical writer to one who could wholeheartedly espouse a political cause. With typical politico-literary logic this critic concluded:

> Even if you began as Hemingway began, with a simple emotional desire to transmit experience, to find and convey the truth, if you follow the truth to its logical conclusion, you will end where Hemingway has ended now, in the People's Front [that is, on the side of leftists/Communists].

Such critics recognized that the explosion in Spain had shocked Hemingway into political action, and these same critics who had once been so irritated with the writer's failure to mainfest a social conscience in his novels, were ready now to reverse their evaluation and welcome him as an "écrivain engagé [politically engaged writer]." [Hemingway biographer] Philip Young comments that Hemingway's political isolationism was not shattered until the actual fighting began in Spain, which "more than anything else seems to have brought him wholly back to the world."

Friends on Both Sides

Hemingway was well acquainted with political developments in Spain. He had followed the Spanish political situation under the monarchy, the establishment of the Republic in 1931, and the reaction during the conservative election victory in 1933. He recognized the faults and virtues of the various political factions contending for control in Spain, but other than being adamantly antifascist, Hemingway refused to take sides in the internal political affairs of the country. By 1936 he was sufficiently knowledgeable to realize the degree of factionalism present in the Spanish Republican government, and the extent to which fascism had influenced the thinking of the reactionary military elements within Spain. Once Italy and Germany had actively entered into the internal affairs of Spain in violation of the nonintervention agreement, Hemingway's old hatred of fascist states and his distrust of the political machinations of European governments furnished justification for his commitment to the Loyalist cause.

The motives behind Hemingway's involvement in the Spanish struggle are contained in a letter which he wrote to Carlos Baker in 1951. In retrospect, Hemingway reflected on his liberal stand:

> There were at least five parties in the Spanish Civil War on the Republican side. I tried to understand and evaluate all five (very difficult) and belonged to none. . . . I had no party but a deep interest in and love for the Republic. . . . In Spain I had, and have, many friends on the other side. I tried to write truly about them, too. Politically, I was always on the side of the Republic from the day it was declared and for a long time before.

With the outbreak of fighting, it was necessary for Hemingway to choose his course of action.

Social Issues in Literature

CHAPTER 2

For Whom the Bell Tolls and War

Hemingway Strived to Write About Truth

Shabnum Iftikhar

Shabnum Iftikhar is a writer for Language in India, *a monthly online journal devoted to the study of the languages spoken in the Indian sub-continent.*

In the following viewpoint, Iftikhar says that Hemingway's experience as a news reporter in the Spanish Civil War enabled him to realistically portray war and its effects in For Whom the Bell Tolls. *Hemingway describes the horror of war, focusing on loss of life and humanity on both sides of the conflict, so that* For Whom the Bell Tolls *is more about war itself than politics. In writing about war on a greater scale, Iftikhar argues, Hemingway attempted to understand the human condition.*

No study of Ernest Hemingway's works can be completed without an understanding of the author's life because he is one of those authors whose life and works are interdependent. In fact, there are three Hemingways: Hemingway the man, Hemingway the author, and Hemingway the legend. It is difficult to say where one ends and the other begins. The author has derived most of his raw material for his novels and short stories from his personal experiences and his books have influenced his life tremendously. Hemingway the author and Hemingway the man produced the legendary Hemingway.

Hemingway: The Man and the Author

As an author, throughout his life, he has captured those realities which he observed from very close quarters. Deep and profound is his knowledge, whether those are the brutalities of Spanish civil war or those are the sufferings of 'Lost Generation' or those are the adventures of matadors in a bull fighting ring. His first-hand knowledge about all these realities has enabled him to portray what is true and to delineate those characters with whom he encountered in real life. Hemingway has had a life, full of diversity. He had been so involved and engrossed in activities such as an ambulance driver, as a news reporter, as an expatriate, as a big game hunter that nothing seems impossible to him when he gives vent to his feelings by taking into account his experiences of life.

The Background of the Novel

"For Whom the Bell Tolls" has been written in the backdrop of Spanish civil war, Hemingway experienced as a news reporter. Therefore, the chances of exaggeration are almost equal to nothing and he leaves no stone unturned to expose the sufferings, the brutalities and the miseries of common human beings. These are some factors that caused him to write "For Whom the Bell Tolls".

The Spanish civil war was fought in 1930s between Fascist and Republicans with an impression that both sides were considering themselves right in their own scenarios. It is a general phenomenon that two opposite forces, involved in a war consider themselves always right and their purpose behind the war. They damn care of how much there is a blood shed and how much there is a loss of humanity on both sides. Hemingway in "For Whom the Bell Tolls" recounts those memories, which were nerve-shattering experiences not only for him, but also for those human beings, who had seen the catastrophe of the 1st world war, were experiencing this in the Spanish civil war and unfortunately were destined to experience this in the form of 2nd world war in the coming years.

The Protagonist of the Novel

Robert Jordan is a protagonist of the novel. The novel narrates what happens in the life of an American volunteer, Robert Jordan, who has been assigned the task of blowing up a bridge in the hills. He goes through the same nerve-shattering experience, when he takes part in the war in actual life. He is on the Republican side, fights against Fascist. He participates in the war with a hope to do something for Republicans. His endurance, determination and persistence have been presented by Hemingway with a unique touch of patriotism. He is a warrior, who is sincere to his cause more than anything else.

What happens to this cause, when with the passage of time, he becomes able to distinguish the difference between appearance and reality and what happens to his determination and sincerity, when he comes to realize that the resulting effects of war are nothing but a massacre and a loss of humanity on a greater scale. This is exactly what Hemingway has been concerned with as an author throughout his life. He is not interested in telling the cock and bull stories, related to bold and audacious adventures of his heroes, rather he describes the inner turmoil, the sufferings and pains, people experience in the name of war. He takes the responsibility on his shoulders to bring to light the hideous sides and heinous aspects of wars, fought in the 20th century. Perhaps no other 20th century writer has been this much involved to capture the inner conflict, the hollowness of minds and the spiritual emptiness of the lost generation, who experienced this entire era and became a lost generation in the long run.

The Concept of a 'Lost Generation'

'Lost Generation' was a term Hemingway made famous by using it permanently in his novels. As a matter of fact, all his protagonists are lost generation, wandering aimlessly in the post-war world without any ambition and without any ray of hope. They cut a sorry figure in terms of moral, social and religious values. They have seen this much destruction and annihilation that their beliefs have been destroyed. They take refuge in drink and sex to forget their miseries, but love and sex have lost their sacredness and their glamour and having the act of sex is just like having a glass of beer or wine. Religion was also on the verge of disaster and those religious values had been declined, which 19th century cherished. They had become the victims of indispensable inner dilapidation. They were all wounded physically, spiritually or psychologically after seeing violence and deaths in its various manifestations.

This is the overwhelming impression of 'Lost Generation', powerful and realistic, Hemingway has created in his works. He has been successful in his juxtaposition of the pre-war and post-war scenarios and values to reveal the adverse effects of war on the minds of his generation. It is not just one war, Hemingway talks about, rather it is a series of wars, he experienced and observed throughout the first fifty years of the previous century. As an acute observer, he was fully aware, how these wars are undermining moral values and social structure of an entire generation and society. The occurrence of these wars was the catalyst that finally created the 'Lost Generation'. Hemingway grabs this opportunity to foment feelings against the war and war effects through his novels.

Confrontation with Nothingness

Hemingway delineates his heroes with unique truthfulness with the strong impression that they are the guys who have confrontation in their lives either with violence or deaths. Nevertheless, they do tireless efforts to achieve their cause and fulfill their tasks assigned to them. In this interim, how much they do suffer and how they do prove themselves indefatigable warriors and how much they do endeavor to complete their onerous assignments, it gives a reader a true account of 20th century war era. Hemingway's pragmatic approach in creating such characters is undoubtedly undeniable. He presents his heroes as obdurate, courageous, loyal to their cause, so what if they are naive and artless.

During the Spanish Civil War Ernest Hemingway (right) served as a correspondent. Here he is talking to Soviet forces in front of a Soviet tank. © Hulton-Deutsch Collection/ Corbis.

Perhaps Hemingway's approach behind these characters is that it's not only experience and armament required to win the war but passion and determination are also required and in this capacity, his heroes show a great amount of zeal. Isn't the irony of life that these courageous and passionate heroes lose all of the charm of their cause, when they do confront the futility of war and experience a feeling of nothingness. As humanity is dying at both sides, they remain indecisive, who is innocent and who is culpable. In 'For Whom the Bell Tolls', if Robert Jordan does confront the same nothingness, how could he justify his cause behind the war he is fighting for. The very inability of Hemingway's heroes leads them eventually to a life of senses: drink, sex and so on. Once determined, audacious and loyal, they become wandering souls with a sense of alienation. To mitigate this sense of alienation, they involve themselves in such activities so much so that they could justify their existence. This is a world, exasperated by the war, Hemingway shows in his novels where his heroes are born and brought up and live their lives in a smug complacency.

Title of the Novel

Hemingway's circumspect approach in choosing the title of the novel is truly matchless. It's not just a title. There can be felt an echo of the present time, years or century. The universality of the title broadens the horizon of the novel.

This bell doesn't toll only for Robert Jordan or for his other heroes. It tolls for every single man who loses his life in a man-made catastrophe, that is, war. On one hand, he does focus on the melancholic lives of his heroes and on the other hand, he seems to strive for this purpose that he could prove his heroes' death purposeful. It can be felt as he had found something for his protagonists to die—a death of dignity, in case of unavailability of dignified life.

Hemingway as a spokesman of the 20th century is at his best, when he transforms the valueless human life into worth-dying death. His novels are the precious contribution to the kernel of American Literature. Hemingway as a representative of the 20th century 'Lost Generation' feels for everyman's death as he was involved with humanity. The world today, is in a dire need of another Hemingway, who could expose the futility of wars, going on in the world and could bring the atrocities of these wars to the forefront, so that no one do feel the need to ask 'For Whom The Bell Tolls', everyone must know, it can toll for thee.

Hemingway Shows All Sides
of War

Peter Messent

Peter Messent has taught American and Canadian studies at the University of Nottingham, England. He is the author of The Cambridge Introduction to Mark Twain *and* Mark Twain and Male Friendship.

Messent observes in the following excerpts that in For Whom the Bell Tolls, *Hemingway moves away from the limited narrative perspectives of his earlier novels. In doing so, he is able to present all sides of the Spanish Civil War and not merely one character's opinions. Hemingway uses interior discourse to present the reader with a wide variety of insights into warfare, and Robert Jordan's interior monologues display his own self-division about the necessity of warfare and its justification. But in the end, Messent argues, Robert Jordan overcomes any sense of uncertainty about his own actions to further the Republican cause, and his heroic individualism is fully realized.*

*F*or Whom the Bell Tolls is one of Hemingway's most popular novels. Robert Jordan shares many of those heroic qualities Hemingway associated with the bullfighter. He too has—or comes to have—knowledge, passion, courage and control. Harry [Morgan], in *To Have and Have Not*, is strongly aware of the determining conditions that limit every aspect of his life and operate to render his strong sense of himself ineffectual. Like so many protagonists in the hard-boiled novel of the 1930s, he is associated with action rather than consistent thought as he looks to survive, physically and economically, in an oppressive world. The reader is also held at one remove from Harry. Questions about ends and means link his illegal activities to those of the Cuban revolutionaries and raise unresolved doubts as to his ultimate status (heroic or otherwise). The narrative techniques used, moreover, remove him more and more from the novel's centre as it proceeds.

Showing All Sides of War

Jordan is much more obviously a heroic figure. The novel closely focuses around him from start to end. Although again there is a strongly deterministic element to the novel in the sense that Robert's fate (and that of the Republican cause) is preordained, he has freely chosen to place himself in this situation and is acting not for himself but with larger ends in mind—for "the future of the human race" may be at stake here. This ability to see any distance beyond the immediate facts of the situation marks him off from previous [Hemingway] protagonists. Robert is a university professor who is associated with a wider outlook and a more consistently reflective intelligence than Harry. The narrative techniques used endorse such differences in that his thoughts and feelings are given in more extended form than those of any prior Hemingway protagonist.

In this novel, Hemingway continues to move away from the limited narrative perspectives of *The Sun Also Rises* and *A Farewell to Arms*. Such a move suits the broadscale intentions of a novel which works outward from Robert's own specific experience to that of the Spaniards with whom he is most directly involved (the members of Pablo's and El Sordo's band and, to lesser extent, Berrendo) to those Republicans and their supporters (both Spanish and foreign) in Madrid and in the military lines. Robert's experience is thus placed in a wider context than that given for Frederic Henry or Nick Adams, Hemingway's previous men at war. When Hemingway had just begun *For Whom the Bell Tolls* he wrote to Ivan Kashkin, the Soviet literary critic whose name he borrows in the novel. Referring to "stories about the war", he says, "I try to show *all* the different sides of it . . . examining it from many ways. So never think one story represents my viewpoint because it is much too complicated for that." In the shift from the short story to the novel form such complications could be tackled. In *A Farewell to Arms* the view of war is a largely one-sided one, necessarily so since Frederic Henry's first-person narration acts as a filter on its presentation.

Multiple Points of View

The larger concern with the meaning of the Spanish civil war, and the political, military and social issues involved, lead now to a complete change of narrative tactics. Thus not only is the narration from an omniscient third-person position but the range of focalisation in the novel is extensive. This produces the odd aberrant effect as, for instance, when Pablo's horse's thoughts are represented, but for the most part is a highly effective way of extending the text's range of voices and positions. So, for example, in the last few pages of chapter 28 and the start of the next chapter, we are given at least eight different perspectives on the action: those of the Fascist sniper, Berrendo, El Sordo, Joaquin, Ignatio, Jordan, Maria and Anselmo. The use of omniscient narration contributes to this sense of breadth. In chapters 34–42 the narrative swings back and forth from Andrés's journey across the lines to division headquarters to the actions of the guerilla band just prior to their attack on the bridge. As the reader follows Andrés toward the front line, switches of focalisation again occur which add to our general understanding of the politics and psychologies of command. André Marty's mentally disturbed condition is revealed as the workings of his own mind are set against his actions and the way others talk about and behave toward him. We follow Duval and Golz's thoughts when they finally receive the dispatch, which reaches them too late for it to influence events. All these devices add to the broad-scale and multi-faceted picture of the war presented.

In this novel, then, the reader is presented with a whole series of larger locating points and frames to the central protagonist's actions. Hemingway's earlier war fiction lacks such contexts. Pilar's long story of what happened in Avila at the start of the revolutionary movement is the type of extended exercise in personal and public history marked by its absence in the earlier texts. It is intended "to complicate Jordan's and the reader's understanding of the ethical responsibility inhering within any particular action" [according to critic James L. Kastely in his article "Toward a Politically Responsible Ethical Criticism: Narrative in *The Political Unconscious* and *For Whom the Bell Tolls*"]. We are also given a much fuller picture of the central protagonist than appears in the earlier texts. David Wyatt [in his book *Prodigal Sons: A Study in Authorship and Authority*] speaks of this novel as being a "long book about a short time" and contrasts it to [Hemingway's short-story collection] *In Our Time* in the fact that "it leaves nothing out". It is he says, with reference to Frederic Henry's earlier activities, "a book that fills rather than kills time". In previous novels the use of unreliable first-person narrators, the number of gaps and inconsistencies in their stories, and the concentration on immediate event and sensation rather than considered reflection were all means of indicating the protagonists' instability and incompleteness. Here Robert is—or at least becomes—a centred, unified and complete self.

Interior Discourse

Hemingway makes much greater use of interior discourse than he does in *The Sun Also Rises* and *A Farewell to Arms*. We get to know Jordan fully from within as he reflects on immediate events but also spirals away mentally from the present to take in a variety of subjects which include his past, his political position, the Spanish people and his relationship to them, and his projected future. Two of the most conspicuous examples of this use of interior discourse occur in chapters 13 and 18. In the former, we are given his thoughts and feelings as he makes love to Maria. The time of the present narrative then comes to a full stop ("because now he was not there") as he thinks about the immediate military situation that confronts him. Jordan goes on to reflect on his effect on the lives of those now being "used" by him for the necessary military ends and to think about the military command in Spain, his own politics and the language in which they were expressed. He then returns to think about Maria, her past and their future. This takes his thoughts back to his present "strange life", forward to the book he wishes to write about it, and back once more to the importance of the present moments; the fullness of his life as he is now leading it. This provides a selection of his thoughts during the brief period in story time before the narrative picks up where it had left off ("and he came back to the girl.") Seven pages of text are given to this representation of his interior discourse. Similarly in chapter 18, Jordan moves mentally away from the immediate problem with Pablo to think about Madrid and Gaylord's. There is an eighteen-page digression from the time of the first narrative as he reflects on what he has learnt about military and political realities in this war and about what Karkov has taught him concerning their complexity. Chapter 19 brings him and the reader sharply back to the narrative present with Maria's "What do you do sitting there?"

The text's extended explorations of the central protagonist's thoughts and feelings is accompanied by a stylistic expansiveness far removed from the taut understatement that is the norm in earlier texts. Such a shift is to be seen in the use of long sentences, of chains of adjectives—"the dry-mouthed, fear-purged, purging ecstasy of battle"—and of extended figurative device (see, for example, the "He did not want to make a Thermopylae [battle in 480 B.C. in which a small band of

Spartan warriors held off the whole Persian army until the Spartans were betrayed and all inevitably killed]" passage). Jordan is fully known to the reader. There are none of the kind of difficulties of interpretation concerning his motivation and psychological position that problematise earlier texts. This is not to say that Robert Jordan is not a complex protagonist, or that he is initially presented as a fully coherent subject. This is far from being the case.

Self-Division About War

For Robert's awareness of his own self-division is highlighted forcefully on two occasions in the novel. In chapter 26, that part of him which knows that killing is inevitable in the context of war engages in dialogue with the part which is aware of the need to guard against taking such killing as "alright" and thus allowing its full meaning to be avoided. The distinctions Jordan juggles with here are narrow, but the sense of a man trying to reconcile potentially contradictory aspects of himself is clear in the two separate voices heard: "Listen, he told himself. . . . Then himself said back to him, You listen, see?" What is noticeable here is that Jordan, as he confronts the moral complexities of his position as part of the book's larger argument about ends and means, is able to reconcile these two voices—to move toward a unity of voice and be-ing—as he works out exactly his position on this issue in rela-tion to his larger set of beliefs: "no man has a right to take another man's life unless it is to prevent something worse happening to other people." Although this statement comes from just one of the voices being represented, the tenor of the ending of the sequence suggests that this is the final position taken on the issue; that this is the voice he wishes to speak for him.

A sharper sense of self-division on Jordan's part occurs to-ward the end of the novel. In chapter 38 he gives way, follow-ing Pablo's apparent desertion, to self-contempt and defeatism. In the next chapter, with Pablo returned, he recovers confidence in himself. He is able to balance his possible death against his shared love with Maria without the one cancelling out the worth of the other. He has confidence now in his ability to complete his task. He refers back, though, to his previous state: "And you, he said to himself . . . you were pretty bad back there. I was ashamed enough of you. . . . Only I was you. . . . We were all in bad shape. You and me and both of us. Come on now. Quit thinking like a schizophrenic. . . . You're all right again now." Again we have the sense of different elements of Robert's self struggling against each other, but in this process such self-divisions are overcome. Jordan recovers confidence here in his ability to channel the self to realise its best potential and to continue to move in the direction of significant and necessary action.

The Capacity for Heroism

The similarities and differences between Frederic Henry and Jordan begin to become evident in such details. Both are caught in a trap. Frederic's is ultimately a biological one while Robert's seems spun by fate and reinforced by political and military circumstance. The stress on the foredoomed nature of Jordan's enterprise is strong from the start with Pablo's question as to whether he would be willing to be left behind if he were wounded in the attack on the bridge and Jordan's own recognition, when Pablo asks him if he wants to die, of the "seriousness" of his position in attempting to carry out his orders: "You can see it and I see it and the woman read it in my hand". There is also here the same kind of attention paid to a larger constraining reality which diminishes individual effort as there was in *A Farewell to Arms*. The strength of the enemy is foregrounded from the first with Pablo's "*They* are very strong." The novel was written when Hemingway already knew that [as Kastely puts it] "the Republic was doomed". The third-person narrator notes that the result of "Andrés's mission" would probably have been the same even if Jordan's message regarding the Fascist preparation for the coming attack had not been held up by Marty—though the later narrative rather cuts against such a judgement. The immediate success of Jordan's mission is compromised by the "famous balls up" of the larger attack.

This does not, however, prevent Jordan from acting forcefully and well to make his part of the mission a success. In this he differs from Frederic who is characterised only by his passivity and whose lack of control over his military environment is apparent in the fact that he is "blown up while we were eating cheese". Heroic action is an impossibility for this maimed and powerless subject whose one autonomous decision is to run away, to make his separate peace. Robert Jordan, in contrast, is not disassociated. He acts forcefully and confidently in the areas open to him to do so. Larger constraints may be present but they do not diminish the possibility of heroic action; of the self acting autonomously and optimistically, within a limited sphere. "The greatest gift that he had", he tells himself, was "that ability not to ignore but to despise whatever bad ending there could be". He judges his behaviour as he goes along—"you have behaved OK. So far you have behaved all right"—and does what Anselmo calls "an enormous work" in the wiring of the bridge. Like the latter, he is "one with all of the battle and with the Republic" as he does so. He fights for his ideals despite his knowledge of all that work against them and still acts on the belief that the things he does "may make all the difference" as he lies awaiting death. Though he recognises that he has been "bitched" by the orders that Golz had been given, he still trusts that "later on we will have these things much better organized". He acts on the principle that what he does can make a difference and, in Hemingway's world, that is the very best one can do. He is a heroic figure who blows up the specified military target. This kind of heroism is not an option open to Frederic Henry, Nick Adams or

Jake Barnes. Their status as (damaged) subjects is presented as inevitable in a world where the capacity for autonomous will and choice and for the active expression of separate selfhood had already been drastically compromised.

A Completely Integrated Hero

Robert Jordan is a very different case. Described as "completely integrated" at the novel's conclusion, his education (to which frequent reference has been made) is by that stage finalised. This *bildungsroman* [novel of personal development] is complete—even if Robert's gains in self-knowledge and his maturation cannot prevent his death. Jordan knows when to act and when it is necessary to stifle those thoughts and emotions that hinder such action. He is, despite the claims of a number of critics to the contrary, both politically knowledgeable and astute. Much of the novel, indeed, concerns the political intricacies and ambivalences of a situation in which Jordan, despite an awareness of the similarities of the combatants, can still fight for the Republic because of his belief in it as a system of government and his knowledge that "if it were destroyed life would be unbearable for all those people who believed in it". Jordan has none of the problems about where to position himself in relation to the secular-religious divide of Jake and Henry. He is able to plumb his personal past, unavailable for purposes of therapy or as a marker of growth to those earlier subjects, and to come to terms with his ambivalent feelings concerning it. He can distinguish between love and duty and does not look to the former as a type of retreat from the social self as does Frederic Henry. Rather he celebrates the "luck" and "value" found in the intensity of that love which gives him a similar sense of the completion of self in the other, but does not let it blind him to what he sees as his social responsibilities. Both go together in his mind as elements of that complete self which he becomes. The strength of Jordan's commitment to life and his determination to live it fully to its last drop can be evidenced in that change of tense in the passage on one of the last pages: 'I hate to leave it. . . . I have tried to [do some good in it] with what talent I had. *Have, you mean. All right, have'*. In Robert Jordan's figure and his thoughts, positive and heroic individualism are fully realised. Any sense of uncertainty on the subject's part is worked through and overcome in the course of the novel.

Hemingway Refused to Write War Propaganda

Jeffrey Meyers

Jeffrey Meyers is a professional writer living in Berkeley, California.

In the following viewpoint, Meyers discusses the parallels between the Peninsular War, a military conflict during the Napoleonic Wars, and the Spanish Civil War, which inspired Hemingway's For Whom the Bell Tolls. *Meyers argues that Hemingway was aware of the parallels between the Peninsular War and the Spanish Civil War and used elements of both to write his famous novel. Although Hemingway was pro-Loyalist,* For Whom the Bell Tolls *is not propaganda, but a realistic war novel. By drawing heavily from the history of two wars, Hemingway created an accurate portrait of war, Meyers concludes.*

When I interviewed Martha Gellhorn for my biography of Hemingway, she told me that he'd been reading General Sir William Napier's History of the War in the Peninsula (1828-40) while writing *For Whom the Bell Tolls* (1940). During the Spanish Civil War Hemingway made three trips to Spain as a journalist and reported the major battles with a novelist's eye. Fascinated by the patriotic fervor he observed in the peasants and workers, he noticed the striking parallels between the Peninsular War and the Civil War. He looked up Napier's eye-witness account, which led him to later histories.

The Peninsular War

The Peninsular War, in the early nineteenth century, was part of the costly and protracted struggle that opposed Napoleon's attempt to conquer Europe. The British, under Wellington,

Jeffrey Meyers, "Hemingway and the Peninsular War," *Notes on Contemporary Literature*, vol. 4, no. 2, March 2012. Copyright © 2010 by Notes on Contemporary Literature. All rights reserved. Reproduced by permission.

joined forces with the Spanish and Portuguese armies, raised the blockade of their ports and drove the French from Spain. This war saw the emergence of guerrillas (Spanish for "little wars"), in which mobile bands of freelance fighters harassed the enemy and helped the allies defeat the French. Ronald Fraser's recently published *Napoleon's Cursed War: Spanish Popular Resistance in the Peninsular War* describes the valuable contribution of these independent fighters.

Like the Peninsular War, the Spanish Civil War was international in scope. Fascist Germany and Italy intervened on the side of General Franco; Communist Russia supported the Loyalists. The volunteers on the Loyalist side came from every country in Europe and joined the militias that were affiliated with various left-wing parties. But there was an important and tragic difference between the earlier and the later wars. In the Peninsular War the guerrillas had a unifying common goal and fought to support the regular armies; in the Civil War the Loyalists were not only overwhelmed by fascist military power, but rival militias also fought amongst themselves and the guerrillas disintegrated into brutal factions.

Hemingway learned of the guerrilla tradition, crucial to the idea of Spanish patriotism, from direct experience as well as from books. Broadcasting on Radio Madrid during the war, La Pasionaria, the famous Loyalist leader and orator, frequently evoked memories of the Spanish rising against Napoleon during the fight for independence in 1808. In *For Whom the Bell Tolls*, his particular blend of action, love story and documentary, Hemingway based the military leaders on real people and the progress of the war on actual events, but focused on how a particular guerrilla group actually fought. He recreated the background, politics and tactics of a heterogeneous guerrilla band, acting independently yet following the orders of the regular army, and invented typically Spanish characters, inspired by men he had known before and during the Spanish Civil War.

Nineteenth-Century Guerrillas

The nineteenth-century guerrillas were small, mobile groups—with internal cohesion, collective identity and esprit de corps—that opposed a static regular army. They included some women; a significant number of outlaws, villains and troublemakers; and a number of foreign conscripts who had deserted from the French army. Most of the guerrillas and their leaders were peasants who had experienced collective violence at the hands of the enemy, "often with personal consequences: the death of close relatives, the abuse of female kin, forced labour in carrying or carting for the occupying army, the forcible seizure of food supplies and an infinity of individual indignities". There were two main kinds of guerrilla bands: "Those who took up arms without any authorization from either civilian or military authorities could be called partisans; those who asked for and received official authorization to create new groups . . . could be termed privateers".

Operating behind enemy lines, the fighters were essentially territorial. The deep gorges, hidden valleys and numerous mountain ranges in Spain were perfect guerrilla country. The French soldiers, trained for the traditional order of battle, were neutralized by the hostile terrain and the surprise attacks. The bands also provided valuable intelligence for their allies: "Small military groups reconnoitered and probed the enemy's lines, seizing prisoners to gain information on their opponents' strength, movements, food supplies and battle plans. . . . It was the first time that the guerrilla became a nationwide form of resistance and a sanctified right of self-defence". In this war, as in the Spanish Civil War, "reprisals on occasion rose to barbarous heights among the opponents in the guerrilla struggle".

At exactly the same time that he was fighting the Peninsular War in Spain, Napoleon rashly invaded Russia. Like the Spanish, the Russians opposed a superior army that had overextended itself into hostile territory. They avoided the con-

War correspondents covering the Spanish Civil War, circa 1937. Ernest Hemingway is to the left of the man with the binoculars. © Hulton-Deutsch Collection/Corbis.

frontation of massive forces in traditional warfare, sanctified by Karl von Clausewitz, and concentrated that unknown quantity, the spirit of the army, in a series of sporadic guerrilla encounters.

For Whom the Bell Tolls and Guerrilla Fighters

As in the Peninsular War, the guerrillas in *For Whom the Bell Tolls* belong to a lawless mobile band that fight against a regular army; include women and foreigners; and recruit peasants who'd been persecuted by the enemy. They gather intelligence, are patriotic and territorial, and operate in a mountainous terrain that is hostile to the fascists. They carry out the same sudden and surprising, probing and withdrawing, hit-and-run attacks, ambush enemy columns and terrorize them in hand-to-hand encounters. They are quite capable of barbaric reprisals.

Hemingway based aspects of Robert Jordan on T.E. Lawrence, who adopted the tactics of his Spanish and Russian predecessors and used them while brilliantly leading the Arab revolt against the Turks in World War I. Both Lawrence and Jordan are foreign technical experts who assume command of a guerrilla group operating behind enemy lines. Both have a scholarly background, have spent many years in the country before the war, and have a sound knowledge of the language and culture of the people they lead. Both adopt the local customs, do not feel like outsiders and are not treated as such. Both take up an alien cause for their own idealistic reasons, destroy trains and bridges by detonating explosives, and are forced to kill their own wounded companions.

In *For Whom the Bell Tolls* hundreds of guerrillas are fighting in the mountains around Madrid. The most important group, led by El Sordo ("the deaf one"), join the attack on the bridge and are wiped out by enemy aircraft. In the novel all the guerrillas are peasants and many—like Pablo and Anselmo—are illiterate. They all dress in black peasant smocks, stiff gray trousers and rope-soled shoes, and Jordan wears the same clothing. They use the familiar form of address, tu instead of usted; call each other camarada (comrade); and say Don and Senor only when they're joking.

Hemingway's Realistic Portrayal of War

Hemingway artfully combines many elements to suggest the difficulty of the undertaking and intensify the suspense. The mission must be timed precisely and Jordan must impose discipline upon the guerrillas, yet the group dynamics conspire against him. Pilar fatalistically prophesies that Jordan will meet his death, and Pablo treacherously undermines the attack. Jordan's love for and sex with Maria arouses Pilar's jealousy and the men's hostility. There is a heavy snowstorm, Pablo steals the detonators and the enemy discovers their plans. The cavalry patrols the area, the bridge is unexpectedly defended and fascist planes drop bombs. El Sordo's band is massacred, and Andreés is unable to deliver Jordan's message warning Golz to cancel his attack. Afterwards, the group finds it difficult to escape to the Gredos mountains.

At the end of the novel, when all Jordan's doubts and fears have been realized, he's forced to launch his "surprise attack" on an enemy who is expecting it. In this battle, the good men—Anselmo, Agustin, Fernando, Andreés, Eladio and Primitivo—are killed. Pablo and Rafael, who look out for themselves, manage to escape with Pilar and Maria. Jordan blows up the bridge, but breaks his leg when his horse is shot by the enemy and falls on him. Like Kashkin, he prefers to die rather than be captured, tortured and executed. He remains behind to kill the fascist Lieutenant Berrendo, who cut off the heads of El Sordo's men, and to be killed by his soldiers. The last sentence of *For Whom the Bell Tolls* leaves Jordan close to the earth but not yet in it: "He could feel his heart beating against the pine needle floor of the forest". It also repeats both the first sentence of the novel, completing the circular unity of the book, and echoes the last sentence of "The Snows of Kilimanjaro": "But she did not hear him for the beating of her heart."

Hemingway was pro-Loyalist but did not write propaganda. Critics on the left attacked his realistic portrait of guerrillas in action. His great novel, which drew on his reading about the Peninsular War as well as on his contemporary reporting in Spain, portrays both the triumphs and failures of the guerrilla war: the idealism and treachery, patriotism and cowardice, courage and brutality, sacrifice and selfishness, comradeship and anarchy, executions and remorse. Hemingway's vision of the world, embodied in Jordan, is essentially idealistic and romantic. He contrasts this view with the peasant cunning of Pablo. Jordan speaks for the author when he reflects on the fighting spirit and conflicting motives of the Spanish peasants. Alluding to Madame de Stael's maxim, "Tout comprendre c'est tout pardonner," Jordan concludes: "There is no finer and no worse people in the world. No kinder people and no crueler. And who understands them? Not me, because if I did I would forgive it all". In the twenty-first century guerrillas continue to pin down and damage well-trained regular armies, and have remained as ruthless, effective and flawed as Hemingway's Spanish fighters.

Hemingway's Characters Fight for a Cause

Peter L. Hays

Peter L. Hays has taught English and American literature at the University of California at Davis. He is the author of several books on Ernest Hemingway.

In the following essay, Hays notes that For Whom the Bell Tolls *marks a progression in the development of the Hemingway hero. In earlier novels, such as* A Farewell to Arms, *Hays writes, the Hemingway hero was suspicious of causes and the abstract words associated with them, words such as "honor" and "duty." And while Hemingway understands that which side one takes in a war is often a matter of geography or chance rather than politics, his Loyalist Spaniards are willing to lay down their lives to fight Fascist oppression. So too, the hero, Robert Jordan, dies for a cause that he believes is the correct one. The novel, Hays observes, is a testament to human courage and a denunciation of war and man's inhumanity to man.*

In October 1940, Hemingway published *For Whom the Bell Tolls* and recouped his standing among critics after it had fallen with [his earlier works] *Death in the Afternoon, The Green Hills of Africa, To Have and Have Not,* and *The Fifth Column. For Whom the Bell Tolls* was enormously successful, selling nearly 200,000 copies by year's end. It is a novel based on the Spanish Civil War of 1936–39, which Hemingway saw as the first act of the free world's fight against Fascism; the defeat of the Republicans by Nationalist, Fascist forces, was very ominous for Hemingway, and by the time the novel was completed and published, World War II had indeed begun in Europe. Like *A Farewell to Arms, For Whom the Bell Tolls* combines a love story, an adventure story, and an attack on war.

The Plot

The basic plot concerns three full days in the life of Robert Jordan, an American, a Spanish instructor at the University of Montana, in Spain and fighting on the Loyalist side. He has been active behind Nationalist lines as a dynamiter, working with guerrilla bands to disrupt Nationalist forces. The Republicans plan an attack through the Guadarrama Mountain range toward Segovia, and Jordan is sent to blow up a bridge over which the Nationalists might send reinforcements. He is guided into the mountains by Anselmo to the band of Pablo, a once-fierce fighter now sinking into drink and fear. Pablo's band contains a gypsy named Rafael, brothers Andrés and Eladio, Primitivo, Fernando, and Augustín. In Pablo's decay, the band is held together by the woman he lives with, Pilar, Hemingway's most fully realized woman character and a marvelous creation by any standards. The last member of the band is Maria, a girl whom the guerrillas rescued after dynamiting a train she was being transported on. Maria was the daughter of a town mayor who had been shot by the Falangists, and Maria had been raped by Nationalist soldiers. She and Jordan fall in love, very promptly—she enters his sleeping bag the night they meet—and although it might be argued that she commits herself to life and love as Catherine does in *A Farewell to Arms*, it is less convincingly an adult act of commitment and more the creation, on Hemingway's part, of a female object of wish fulfillment.

Artificial Loyalties and Futile Efforts

Throughout the novel, Hemingway makes it clear that alignment with an army is frequently less a matter of political choice than of geography or chance of employment. A Spanish young man had to join the union in order to get a job as a streetcar conductor; thus the Nationalists considered him a labor radical and executed him and his wife. Once an army controls a territory, all within that area must belong to that army or die, regardless of personal beliefs. Similarly, although Hemingway was sympathetic with the Loyalist, Republican cause, he attacks the brutality on both sides and the absurdity of war as an institution.

The Spanish Civil War was the first mechanized, modern war that involved the wholesale terrorization and destruction of civilians, the German bombing of Guernica (the inspiration of [Spanish artist Pablo] Picasso's painting [of the same name]) being only the most notorious example. Maria's crime, the reason for her parents' execution and her multiple rape, was the party her father belonged to. Andrés, crossing the lines to deliver a message from Jordan, encounters both anarchists who would rather kill him than talk with him, and officers who think that since he comes from Fascist territory, he must be a Fascist. In one of the most riveting, and revolting, sections of the novel, Hemingway has Pilar recount Pablo's taking of their common village. First he lays siege to the military barracks and, after capturing it, executes all survivors. Then he organizes all Loyalists in the village into two lines extending from city hall to a cliff at the edge of the city's plaza, the men in the lines holding flails, pruning hooks, and clubs. His plan is to force the Fascists, defined as store- and landowners, through the gauntlet, to be beaten and then tossed off the cliff, so that all men in the town share in the guilt of their executions. The military strike degenerates into butchery, and that brutality is then revisited on the Republicans when the Nationalists retake the town three days later. Pablo also blinds a captured policeman to make guarding him easier, yet that is the side Jordan is fighting on, for the sake of justice and liberty. Jordan, himself, although he comes to help the Loyalists, realizes that while his presence may be of ultimate benefit (might have been if the Loyalists had won), he is often a source of immediate harm. As a guerrilla, Jordan realizes that

> you stayed with a peasant and his family. You came at night and ate with them. In the day you were hidden and the next night you were gone. You did your job and cleared out. The next time you came that way you heard that they had been shot. It was as simple as that.

At the end of the novel, Jordan realizes that the Rebels know of the Loyalists' impending attack and sends Andrés to call off what will be a futile waste of life. But Andrés encounters so much stupidity, ignorance, bureaucratic inefficiency, and personal one-upmanship at the cost of cooperation that he is delayed until the very start of the battle, and then no one in the vicinity has the authority to call off the worthless attack without getting Madrid's approval, and there isn't time to do that. Meanwhile, Pablo kills fellow Republicans, allies in the attack on the bridge, so that his band will have enough horses to escape, extra horses they no longer need since several of their number have been killed. Thus Jordan and others in the band give their lives for the cause, nobly, but futilely, and Hemingway scathingly indicts the conduct of both sides, as of war itself.

Hemingway's Realism

Also wonderful in the novel is the sense that Hemingway gives that his characters are speaking Spanish throughout, which the author is giving the reader in an accented translation. Literally translating, Hemingway gives the reader "thous" and "thees," as well as "you," distinguishing between colloquial and formal address; he also gives the reader slightly stilted dialogue, but one with remarkable rhythms:

> "This is shameful. I have nothing against him but such a spectacle must terminate." So he walked down the line and pushed through to where Don Federico was standing and

said, "With your permission," [Spanish *con permiso*] and hit him a great blow alongside the head with a club.

"If I were in the ring with [a bull] now I do not know if I could dominate my legs."

"I will respond for thy material."

Similarly, Hemingway makes an advantage of the era's restriction on the publication of certain four-letter words and gives a sense of great exoticism to the swearing, by quoting some in Spanish, translating some portions literally, but substituting "obscenity" for the actual term in others. For example: "I besmirch the milk of thy duty. . . . I obscenity in the milk of thy tiredness. . . . I befoul myself in the milk of the springtime." And again he twice attempts to capture in prose the rhythm and the tension and release of intercourse, the first passage ending with the much-quoted line about the earth moving.

Although Jordan is given to long and garrulous passages of stream-of-consciousness reminiscence and reflection, many passages in the novel are among the best prose Hemingway ever wrote. He makes the gypsy Rafael describe the dynamiting of a train, and he keeps the language at Rafael's uneducated level, yet marvelously descriptive:

> The train was coming steadily. We saw it far away. And I had an excitement so great I cannot tell it. . . . Then it came chu-chu-chu-chu-chu-chu steadily larger and larger and then, at the moment of the explosion, the front wheels of the engine rose up and all of the earth seemed to rise in a great cloud of blackness and a roar and the engine rose high in the cloud of dirt . . . and then it fell onto its side like a great wounded animal and there was an explosion of white steam before the clods of the other explosion had ceased to fall on us and the *máquina* [machine gun] commenced to speak "Ta! Ta! Tat! Tat! Tat! Ta!"

Pilar's whole description of Pablo's attack on her village and her account of the smell of death, as well as Hemingway's narrative of the death of Sordo, another guerrilla leader, are all tours de force [masterful creations], superb examples of narrative, too long to quote here in their entireties, but comparable to Rafael's account in excellence. Another prose technique well handled is the intercutting of chapters between Jordan and the partisans at the bridge and Andrés's attempt to reach Loyalist headquarters. Will Andrés get there in time to prevent the attack, will Jordan have to blow the bridge with makeshift equipment, will there be enough of them to subdue the guard posts? Almost cinematically, Hemingway cuts back and forth between the two events, heightening tension by progressively shortening Andrés's chapters.

Women and Men

As I have said, the conversion of Maria from ravaged victim to dedicated lover is abrupt and, on retrospect, unconvincing. In context, however, Hemingway almost makes the reader believe; he marvelously reestablishes Maria's innocence when he has her say to Jordan that she would like to kiss him but does not know how: "Where do the noses go? I have always wondered where the noses would go?" He individualizes each of the characters, distinguishing the foul-mouthed Agustín from the pompous Fernando; he shows the dignity of an old man like Anselmo who delights in hunting animals, but who cries when he must shoot his fellow man, even though they are the enemy; he scrutinizes the courage of Andrés, the "bulldog of Villaconejos" and through Andrés of all men: Andrés is always first in attacking the bull in his village's amateur bullfights, but he is secretly relieved to be delivering a message for Jordan rather than attacking the bridge. And Hemingway makes Pilar fully dimensional, strong, where Pablo is weak, yet tender toward him, pushing Maria into Jordan's sleeping bag for the girl's sake, knowing that she must love to become whole again, and yet jealous of Maria's beauty and of the happiness of the young lovers. Her complexity is marvelously repre-

Ingrid Bergman (as Maria) and Gary Cooper (as Robert Jordan) in a scene from the 1943 film version of For Whom the Bell Tolls. © INTERFOTO/Alamy.

sented. Through Pablo's default, she is the band's leader. When the partisans agree to help Jordan, in spite of Pablo's objections, she tells him:

> "Here I command! Haven't you heard *la gente* [the people]? Here no one commands but me. You can stay if you wish and eat of the food and drink of the wine, but not too bloody much, and share in the work if thee wishes. But here I command."

This role reversal is taking place, let me insist again, in 1930s' conservative, Catholic Spain, where a woman's place was explicitly defined as secondary to the male's. Later, she takes Jordan and Maria to meet El Sordo, where they encounter Joaquín, a nineteen-year-old failed bullfighter. Teasing him, Pilar says:

> "And if Maria kisses thee again I will commence kissing thee myself. It's years since I've kissed a bullfighter, even an unsuccessful one like thee. . . . Hold him, *Inglés*, till I get a good kiss at him."
>
> "*Deja* [leave it]" the boy said and turned away sharply. . . .
>
> "At times many things tire me," Pilar said angrily. "You understand? And one of them is to have forty-eight years. You hear me? Forty-eight years and an ugly face. Another is to see panic in the face of a failed bullfighter of Communist tendencies when I say, as a joke, I might kiss him."

Commitment to Cause

Pilar also embodies, and makes most explicit, dedication and commitment to a cause. In contrast to *A Farewell to Arms* and Hemingway's comments about the obscenity of abstract words such as *honor* or *courage*, abstract terms such as *duty*, *freedom*, and *liberty* are frequent in *For Whom the Bell Tolls*, as well as examples of the need—not for the independence and self-reliance of a Jake Barnes [protagonist of *The Sun Also Rises*]— but for the interdependence and human solidarity of those fighting together for a common cause, recognizing that a man alone has no chance and that no man is an island entire unto himself. Pilar was for years the companion of Finito, a short, tubercular bullfighter, so short, in fact, that he was almost always hit by a bull's horns when he went in for the kill; he knew he would be hit with the flat of the bull's horns as the bull charged by, yet he killed the bull calmly, accepting the inevitable pain and, ostensibly, ultimately dying from the repeated injuries to his chest. Pilar eulogizes him thus:

"He was short of stature and he had a thin voice and much fear of bulls. Never have I seen a man with more fear before the bullfight and never have I seen a man with less fear in the ring. You," she said to Pablo. "You are afraid to die now. You think that is something of importance. But Finito was afraid all the time and in the ring he was like a lion."

Pilar is part gypsy and skillful at palm reading. She reads Jordan's palm and sees death there as a result of the mission they will undertake. (It isn't important whether Hemingway believed in palm reading; it is important that the gypsy Pilar believes her own gifts, and the way she acts as a result.) In spite of her belief that Jordan and the mission are doomed, and possibly herself as well, she pushes Maria at Jordan, commits herself and the men in her band to Jordan's mission: "'I am for the Republic,' the woman of Pablo said happily. 'And the Republic is the bridge'". Later, Maria tells Jordan, "The Pilar told me that we would all die tomorrow and that you know it as well as she does and that you give it no importance. She said this not in criticism but in admiration."

Tragic Figures

The Hemingway code includes doing what one can as well as one can, regardless of what befalls one, with skill, determination, and craftsmanship. This is what Pilar admires in Jordan, and she displays the same qualities even more herself. Initially Jordan is not pessimistic about his chances, but after the death of Sordo, he grows increasingly so, and thinks about his grandfather's courage fighting in the American Civil War and against the Indians thereafter; he also thinks of his father's suicide, and how he himself will measure up to his forebears. Ultimately, he demonstrates the courage that Pilar has modeled for him.

At one point in the novel a Nationalist cavalryman rides into the guerrillas' camp, and Jordan shoots him. Reading the boy's letters, Jordan discovers him to be from [the town of]

Tafalla, "twenty-one years old, unmarried, and the son of a blacksmith. . . . I've probably seen him run through the streets ahead of the bulls at the Feria in Pamplona, Robert Jordan thought. You never kill any one that you want to kill in a war." The boy has sewn on his uniform the Sacred Heart of Jesus, given him by his sister, who insists that it has been "proven innumerable . . . times to have the power of stopping bullets." Of course it doesn't stop Jordan's, and Maria accuses him of having shot at it. Both sides pray to the same God, same Virgin, same saints. Joaquín, when Sordo's band is attacked, begins spouting Communist slogans and then shifts to prayer. The Nationalist officer, Paco Berrendo, who administers the coup de grace to Joaquín, "made the sign of the cross and then shot him in the back of the head." Hemingway makes Berrendo intelligent, religious, and human. And although it revolts him, Berrendo then cuts off the heads of Sordo's troop as evidence of their death. At the end of the novel, Jordan, lying behind a tree with his leg broken, has Paco Berrendo in his gunsights.

By concentrating the events of the novel into three days, Hemingway strove for the compression of Greek tragedy and, for the most part, achieved it. *For Whom the Bell Tolls* is a great novel of romance and war; a paean to enjoying life while one can, for the time of everyone is limited; a testimony to human courage; and a denunciation of war and man's inhumanity to man. And, published as it was in 1940, a year after World War II had begun in Europe, it was his trumpet call to Americans in the battle against Fascism.

For Whom the Bell Tolls Is a Novel About How to Die

Scott Donaldson

Scott Donaldson is the Louise G.T. Cooley Professor of English, Emeritus, at the College of William and Mary. His many books include Fool for Love, F. Scott Fitzgerald; Hemingway vs. Fitzgerald: The Rise and Fall of a Literary Friendship *and* Fitzgerald and Hemingway: Works and Days.

Hemingway's preoccupation with death in For Whom the Bell Tolls, *Donaldson writes in the following selection, is suggested not only in the novel's title but also in its alternate title, which was* The Undiscovered Country, *a reference to death in Shakespeare's* Hamlet. *Hemingway presents the reader with numerous examples of how to die, in the massacre scene, and in the characterizations of the Russian journalist Karkov, the bomb expert Kashkin, Jordan's lover Maria, and others. Donaldson suggests that Hemingway comes out strongly against suicide, for Jordan's cowardly father had committed this act, which haunts the protagonist up until his own death. Jordan ultimately weighs all of these responses to death, Donaldson says, and faces his own end with dignity.*

*F*or Whom the Bell Tolls *traces the painful education, tele-scoped into three short days, of its protagonist Robert Jordan. From Maria, he learns what it is to love. From Pilar and Anselmo, he learns what it is to belong to a family. Finally he learns in triumph how to die, the most difficult lesson of all and one which he must master on his own.

Scott Donaldson, *By Force of Will: The Life and Art of Ernest Hemingway.* New York: Viking Press, 1977, pp. 299–302. Copyright © 1977 by Scott Donaldson. All rights reserved. Reproduced by permission.

Examples of How to Face Death

The novel stands as an in-depth study of death, a theme reflected not only in its title but in Hemingway's alternate title, "The Undiscovered Country" from whose bourn no traveler returns [as Shakespeare's *Hamlet* puts it]. Early in *For Whom the Bell Tolls*, Pilar "reads" Jordan's imminent death in his palm; after that, the issue becomes not whether Jordan will die, but how. To understand the point, Hemingway continually presents his protagonist, the Spanish literature teacher from Montana who has come to fight for the Loyalists as a demolition expert, with examples of the way others have faced death.

This is one function served by Pilar's long and detailed account of how the mob, led by Pablo, massacred the fascists of their village. Some die well, some do not. Don Benito, the mayor, takes his blows and his fall into oblivion without comment. The brave Don Ricardo defies his persecutors, cursing and spitting at them before they club him to death. The cowardly Don Faustino, on the other hand, dies in humiliation, begging for mercy on his knees, and his example turns the mob ugly and robs the succeeding fascists—even relatively good men like Don Guillermo—of the chance "to be killed quickly and with dignity."

In another scene, El Sordo's last hopeless battle against the fascists, Hemingway once more draws a distinction between dying well and dying badly. Trapped atop a hill, with a superior force surrounding him below and airplanes bringing certain death from above, El Sordo does not fear death, though he hates to give up the joys of living. He fights to the end, firing in futility at the death-dealing planes. El Sordo's dignity and bravery are contrasted here with the prideful stupidity of the fascist Captain Mora, who is tricked into believing that all the Loyalists atop the hill have been killed and so presents himself as a target for Sordo's guns.

Death by Suicide

The kind of death most meticulously explored in the novel is death by suicide: appropriately enough, for at the end Jordan will face, and conquer, the temptation to take his own life. In the abstract, and under the extraordinary pressures of war, Hemingway makes no brief against self-destruction. Maria asks Jordan to teach her how to use a pistol, so that "either one of us could shoot the other and himself, or herself, if one were wounded and it were necessary to avoid capture." She has already had instruction from Pilar on how to cut the carotid artery with a razor blade in the event of capture, and though she's prepared to use the razor blade if need be, she would rather have Jordan shoot her. He promises to do so, though troubled by her matter-of-fact willingness to embrace death.

In the cynical Russian journalist Karkov, he encounters a similar attitude. Karkov has been ordered to poison three wounded Russians and obliterate all evidence of their nationality, in case the fascists take Madrid. But it "isn't so simple just suddenly to poison people," Jordan objects. "Oh, yes it is," Karkov replies, "when you carry it always for your own use"; and he shows Jordan the double suicide kit he carries, one poison capsule in his cigarette case, the other under his lapel, where he could bite and swallow it even if bound. Karkov is no defeatist, he insists, he has simply prepared himself against the possibility of capture.

The Example of Kashkin

But it is another Russian, Kashkin, whose situation most closely matches Jordan's. Also a bomb expert, he works with the guerrillas in blowing up trains; then, when he is wounded and faces capture, he persuades Jordan to shoot him and take him out of his misery. Earlier Kashkin had grown "jumpy" in combat, and extracted a fatalistic promise from Pablo to kill him if wounded. Jordan understands that you "can't have people around doing this sort of work and talking like that." So he rejects out of hand Pablo's suggestion, early in the book, that he might require a similar service:

> "And you," Pablo said. "If you are wounded in such a thing as this bridge, you would be willing to be left behind?"
>
> "Listen," Robert Jordan said and, leaning forward, he dipped himself another cup of the red wine. "Listen to me clearly. If ever I should have any little favors to ask of any man, I will ask him at the time."

At the end, of course, Jordan *is* wounded and cannot escape the fascist troops, but, unlike Kashkin, he turns down Agustín's well-intentioned offer to kill him. That, he knows, would be equivalent to committing suicide, and he has his own reasons for not taking that step—reasons stemming from a family heritage which parallels Hemingway's own.

Jordan's Family History

While the origins of Jake Barnes and Frederic Henry, the protagonists of Hemingway's first two novels [*The Sun Also Rises* and *A Farewell to Arms*, respectively], are left purposely indistinct, Robert Jordan's background is far more clearly sketched. He is the grandson of a cavalry officer in the Civil War and the Indian wars who fought bravely and who with his tales had started Robert reading and studying about war when he was only a boy. In Ernest's case, both grandparents had fought for the Union. Grandfather Hall, an English immigrant, carried a Confederate Minié-ball [type of bullet] in his body to the end of his days, and indignantly refused a government pension from his adopted country for his service in the war. But it was Grandfather Hemingway, a pillar of the G.A.R. [Grand Army of the Republic, a Union army veterans organization] and speechmaker in the schools on Decoration Day, who awoke Ernest's abiding interest in war with a combination of patriotic rhetoric and irreverent war stories.

In this illustration by Orest Vereisky for an edition of For Whom the Bell Tolls, *characters face death by execution.* © RIA Novosti/Alamy.

Jordan's parents are obviously modeled on Dr. and Mrs. Hemingway. His father, like Hemingway's, shot himself with a Smith and Wesson Civil War pistol, and without undergoing the intolerable wartime circumstances that make it possible for Jordan to contemplate the act more or less dispassionately. Maria, Karkov, Kashkin are all faced with the certainty of torture if captured—but Jordan's father had died without that excuse. Under questioning from Pilar, Jordan allows her to think that his father, as a Republican in the United States, faced the same fate that confronted Republicans in Spain:

"And is thy father still active in the Republic?" Pilar asked.

"No. He is dead."

"Can one ask how he died?"

"He shot himself."

"To avoid being tortured?" the woman asked.

"Yes," Robert Jordan said. "To avoid being tortured."

Then Maria looks at him with tears in her eyes, for her own father could not obtain a weapon and so was subjected to brutal physical torture by the fascists. "I am very glad," she says, "that your father had the good fortune to obtain a weapon." Yes, Jordan responds, "it was pretty lucky." Then, to drop a subject which he never brings up again except in dialogue with himself, "Should we talk about something else?"

Jordan is ashamed of his father "because if he wasn't a coward he would have stood up to that woman and not let her bully him." On the eve of the climactic morning when the bridge must be blown, his mind takes him back to memories of his grandfather and his father. Suppose, he thinks, that the four years of the Civil War and then the Indian fighting had used up his grandfather's supply of courage and so he had none left to bequeath and made a *cobarde* [coward] out of his father the way second-generation bullfighters almost always were. But that speculation leads him to a topic he would rather ignore. It was pleasant thinking of his grandfather, but "thinking of his father had thrown him off. He understood his father and he forgave him everything and he pitied him but he was ashamed of him." You'd "have to be awfully occupied with yourself," he thinks, "to do a thing like that."

Facing Death Bravely

Yet on the next day, as Robert Jordan lies in excruciating pain, it is the memory of his father's cowardice and his grandfather's courage which steels him against taking his own life. Soon, he knows, the fascist troops will come bringing certain death, and before he will succumb Jordan is determined to put up a battle with his submachine gun. Maybe, he thinks, he can hold up the fascists a while and help Maria and Pilar and the others escape. But mostly he is motivated against suicide by his father's bad example: "Oh, let them come, he said. I don't want to do that business that my father did. I will do it all right but I'd much prefer not to have to. I'm against that . . . The pain had started suddenly with the swelling after he had moved and he said, Maybe I'll just do it now. I guess I'm not awfully good at pain. Listen, if I do that now you wouldn't misunderstand, would you? *Who are you talking to?* Nobody, he said. Grandfather, I guess. No. Nobody."

But if not his grandfather, then it is Jordan whom Jordan must prove himself to. So he fights back the agony and lasts until the fascist lieutenant rides into range and he can start the fire-fight which will relieve all his pain and enable him to take death, like El Sordo, "as an aspirin."

Pilar's Massacre Story Depicts the Brutality of Humankind

Allen Josephs

Allen Josephs is University Research Professor at the University of West Florida and past president of the Ernest Hemingway Foundation and Society. His books include Ritual and Sacrifice in the Corrida: The Saga of Cesar Rincon.

In the following excerpt, Josephs examines one of the most important passages in For Whom the Bell Tolls, *Pilar's tale of the massacre of Fascists that was led by her husband, Pablo. The inclusion of this passage angered those on the political left, who believed that Hemingway was criticizing the Spanish Republican forces. Hemingway responded by saying that the massacre was based on actual events. But Josephs suggests that Hemingway invented most of the details to fit his fictional needs. Hemingway was showing, Josephs states, that the death of anyone diminishes everyone else, as stated in the epigraph to the novel from which the title is taken. The massacre scene is not a political statement, Josephs argues, but instead functions as a microcosm of the entire tragic Spanish Civil War.*

In chapter ten [of *For Whom the Bell Tolls*], Pilar, Robert Jordan, and Maria go to see El Sordo. Pilar stops along the way to wash her feet in a stream and tell her horrible and fascinating tale of "the day of revolution in a small town where all know all in the town and always have known all." The revolution takes place in a nameless Castilian village possibly somewhere near Avila [in central Spain], the intentionally nameless home of Pablo (and possibly of Pilar, too, although Pilar's actual provenance or even province are never really pinned down). The revolution in Pablo's town clearly stands for conflict in any and all such small towns involved in the violent and unyielding class struggle so central to the Spanish Civil War (Spain had had no class war such as the French Revolution).

A Real or Invented Massacre?

This scene of brutal massacre—committed by those on the side of the Republic—drew heavy fire from the political Left in the U.S. and was interpreted as a traitorous depiction of events. At the meeting with the Veterans of the Abraham Lincoln Brigade [Americans who fought for the Spanish Republic], Hemingway defended himself, claiming, according to Alvah Bessie [an American novelist, journalist, and screenwriter who was blacklisted and jailed as a Communist sympathizer by the House Un-American Activities Committee], that it "was a true incident of the war."

Was it a "true incident of the war"? As is so often the case, the answer is both yes and no. Hemingway apparently told [his friend and biographer A.E.] Hotchner in 1954, "When Pilar remembers back to what happened in their village when the Fascists came, that's Ronda [site of a real massacre], and the details of the town are exact." Hugh Thomas judges Hemingway's description as "near to the reality of what happened in the famous Andalusian town of Ronda (though the work was the responsibility of a gang from Málaga). There 512 were murdered in the first month of the war."

Hemingway clearly had privileged access to many of the horror stories of the war. He knew about Ronda, and he certainly knew of the massacres by the Nationalists in the bullring at [the western Spanish city of] Badajoz because [*Chicago Tribune* reporter] Jay Allen, who reported the story, was a close friend. In the early stages of the war some nearly unimaginable massacres occurred on both sides. Bessie's notion that such massacres were "extremely sporadic in Republican territory" and that they were the "policy of the fascist forces," sounds ingenuous at best. The grand old dean of Hispanophiles [lovers of Spain], Gerald Brenan, may have had the last word when he commented on the Andalusian town of Guadix where young terrorists committed many murders, only to be followed by even fiercer Nationalist purges at the end of the war: "One may take it as a rule that in class wars it is the side that wins that kills most."

Hotchner's report notwithstanding, the details of the town are far from exact. In fact the only real similarities between Ronda and the town of the novel's massacre are the cliff and the river below, a magnificent site that Hemingway obviously found perfect, even though it meant transferring it—as with María and Pilar—from Andalucía to Castilla. Hemingway was probably more accurate about what he actually did when he described the process years later (1954) to his friend Bernard Berenson:

> We are old enough to try to talk truly and I tell you this only as a curiosity. A few other things which I *invented completely* such as the story in "For Whom the Bell Tolls" of Pablo and Pilar and their doing away with the fascists in the village, I read, when by chance I have to do it, with complete astonishment that I could have *invented it* as I did. You know that fiction, prose rather, is possibly the roughest trade of all in writing. . . . You have the sheet of blank paper, the pencil, and *the obligation to invent truer than things can be true.* You have to take what is not palpable and make it completely palpable and also have it seem normal and so that it can become a part of the experience of the person who reads it.

The Massacre Scene Interpreted

The finest critical interpretations of this palpable episode come from [critics] Robert E. Gajdusek and H.R. Stoneback. Gajdusek has examined the moment of revolution in the light of the philosophy of [German philosopher Friedrich] Nietzsche and the psychology of [psychiatrist Carl] Jung as the

Katina Paxinou as Pilar in the 1943 film adaptation of For Whom the Bell Tolls. ©
INTERFOTO/Alamy.

overthrow of the masculine, solar, authoritarian, Apollonian
forces [of order] by the feminine, lunar, revolutionary, Diony-
sian [forces of chaos] uprising. He describes this process as a

> destructive activity that is coevally [at the same time] cre-
> ative . . . a fertility ritual in which fertility is assured through

the separation of the chaff from the wheat, through the threshing and harvesting rituals in which the act of killing with sickle and scythe, or turning or tumbling with a wooden pitchfork, is part of a death process out of which comes renewed life.

Gajdusek's article reveals great complexity of construction, and the deep psychological implications he sees in this "tale" argue very strongly for an intentional, and therefore invented, structure.

Stoneback's piece concerns the price paid in human suffering for the revolution and centers on the figure of the priest, the only priest in the novel, "as the real focus of the tale ... for Pilar in the act of telling, for Pablo in the act of participating and for Hemingway in the precisely crafted act of writing." Even for Pablo, "who hates priests worse than he hates fascists," or perhaps because of that, "everything, the very essence of Spain, is at stake in the death of a Spanish priest." Stoneback believes Pilar's tale, as indeed "everything in *For Whom the Bell Tolls*, conspires to affirm and to take the reader to the heart of [English poet John] Donne's meditation." The epigraph of the novel is "not at all concerned with some superficial leftist vision of brotherhood ... but with the core Christian vision of the oneness of humankind and the relationship of the individual soul to fate." It is important, I believe, to hear Stoneback on this matter. Pablo knows even in his drunken stupor (and that is why he drinks), and Pilar knows (and that is why she recounts) the truth of the epigraph, that regardless of the necessities of war, as Stoneback phrases it, "every death diminishes everyone, and the complicity, for all of Spain and for everyone involved spreads beyond mere knowing, demands—as that rare Christian Anselmo insists—expiation and penance."

Here is Stoneback's conclusion, well worth our consideration:

As George Orwell observed in [his book on the Spanish Civil War] *Homage to Catalonia*: "The sin of nearly all left-wingers from 1933 onwards is that they have wanted to be anti-Fascist without being anti-totalitarian." As Pilar's tale demonstrates, Hemingway does not commit that sin in *For Whom the Bell Tolls*. The novel's ultimate vision approaches that profound and elusive, tragic and redemptive knowledge which declares the need for expiation in the life of communities and nations, a need which has been promulgated in and by all of the outrageous and paradoxical Tiananmen Squares [in Beijing, China, where soldiers killed hundreds of protesters in June 1989] of our bloody century. In Madrid as in Beijing, in all places and times and most especially in our century so ravaged by politics, our epoch so devastated by statism, murderous dogmatism, and isms of every kind, the free, volitional act of resistance to the gnostic rage of ideology—of the left or of the right—must be linked, as Anselmo and Pilar and Hemingway know, as [Russian political prisoner and author Aleksandr] Solzhenitsyn and certain contemporary Chinese writers know, with communal sacraments of atonement.

As if to prove Stoneback's point, Pablo, remembering his victims later, will say, "If I could restore them to life, I would."

The Massacre as Microcosm

Far from Alvah Bessie's simplistic claim in 1970 that "The Spanish war was one of the purest and most easily understood conflicts of modern times," Hemingway's profound understanding of that complex conflict and of its historically gruesome scapegoatism prefigured and shaped his "obligation to invent truer than things can be true." It was never, for Hemingway the novelist, a question of propaganda or the correct political posture. To the extent that Gajdusek and Stoneback are right, Pilar's tale not only "represents the working out of certain spiritual and political dilemmas which gave him great anguish in the late 1930s," it actually incarnates in an intentionally grisly and realistic fashion some of the novel's deepest psychological and spiritual insights, insights that are underscored precisely by virtue of their occurrence on the "wrong" side. To see the scene as politics—or as sensationalism—misses the whole point. It is, as [critic Angel] Capellán has remarked, "a supra-reality, a symbolic—but not less realistic—expression of the tragedy of the Spanish Civil War."

Beautifully phrased, almost poetic at times, and always grim in its realism and taurine [bull-like] symbolism (not unlike [Spanish painter Pablo] Picasso's [famous mural] *Guernica*), Pilar's tale also becomes a self-conscious and intentional analogue for the novel as a whole. Cruelty and drunkenness and shame and the unruly animal of mob behavior—with their precise counterpoint in Jordan's account of the Ohio lynching of the black man—belong to no one group or to no one nation's patrimony. Jordan thinks, going up to the camp of El Sordo, "Pilar had made him see it in that town. If that woman could only write. He would try to write it and if he had luck and could remember it perhaps he could get it down as she told it. God, how she could tell a story. She's better than [sixteenth-century Spanish author Francisco de] Quevedo, he thought." He is inviting us—unintentionally from his own point of view, but intentionally from Hemingway's—to experience the novel as he has experienced Pilar's tale, seeing it as though we had actually been present.

For Whom the Bell Tolls
Is a War Epic

Carlos Baker

Carlos Baker was an American writer, biographer, and professor of literature at Princeton University. Best known as the official biographer of Hemingway, he is the author of numerous books, including Ernest Hemingway: A Life Story *and* Ernest Hemingway: Selected Letters, 1917–1961.

Baker in the following excerpt outlines the ways in which Hemingway's For Whom the Bell Tolls *functions as epic literature, similar to Homer's* Iliad *in its treatment of war. While Hemingway once stated that poor writers embraced and inevitably failed at the epic form, Baker suggests that Hemingway himself succeeded. One of Hemingway's strengths lies in how he uses the holding of the bridge as a microcosm of the larger battle, the war itself, the struggles of Europe and, ultimately, the entire civilized world. Thus, holding a bridge is a single action that has universal meaning. In* For Whom the Bell Tolls, *Baker concludes, Hemingway has adapted the epic form to the needs of the modern reader.*

The structural form of *For Whom the Bell Tolls* has been conceived with care and executed with the utmost brilliance. The form is that of a series of concentric circles with the all-important bridge in the middle. The great concentration which Hemingway achieves is partly dependent on his skill in keeping attention focussed on the bridge while projecting the reader imaginatively far beyond that center of operations. Chapter One immediately establishes the vital strate-

Carlos Baker, *Hemingway: The Writer as Artist*. Princeton, NJ: Princeton University Press, 1952, pp. 245–50. © 1952 Princeton University Press, 1956. 2nd. Edition 1980, renewed in author's name. Reprinted by permission of Princeton University Press.

gic importance of the bridge in the coming action. Frequent allusions to the bridge keep it in view through the second chapter, and in Chapter Three Jordan goes with Anselmo to make a preliminary inspection. From that time onwards until its climactic destruction, the bridge continues to stand unforgettably as the focal point in the middle of an ever widening series of circles.

The Bridge at the Center of History

The brilliance of execution becomes apparent when the reader stands in imagination on the flooring of the bridge and looks in any direction. He will see his horizons lifting by degrees towards a circumference far beyond the Guadarrama mountains. For the guerrillas' central task, the blowing of the bridge, is only one phase of a larger operation which Hemingway once called "the greatest holding action in history." Since the battle strategy which requires the bridge to be destroyed is early made available to the reader, he has no difficulty in seeing its relation to the next circle outside, where a republican division under General Golz prepares for an attack. The general's attack, in turn, is enough to suggest the outlines of the whole civil war, while the [German] Heinkel bombers and [Italian] Fiat pursuit planes which cut across the circle—foreign shadows over the Spanish earth—extend our grasp one more circle outwards to the trans-European aspect of the struggle. The outermost ring of the circle is nothing less than the great globe itself. Once the Spanish holding operation is over, the wheel of fire will encompass the earth. The bridge, therefore—such is the structural achievement of this novel—becomes the hub on which the "future of the human race can turn." Wherever the reader moves along the circumferences of the various circles, all radial roads lead to and from this bridge.

If the reader of *For Whom the Bell Tolls* is hardly cramped for space, he is also free to range in time. Jordan's action, particularized though it is, has also a significance *sub specie aeter-*

nitatis [under the aspect of eternity]. The timelessness of the central event invites the reader to compare it with all those other small and local holding actions which are stuck like gems in the web of history and tend to assume an importance out of all proportion to their size. One civil war easily suggests another, as in Jordan's memories of his grandfather who bore arms in America's war of the rebellion. Behind that, in the long perspective, is the bridge where the republican (and anti-monarchist) "peasants" of Concord [Massachusetts] fired the shot heard round the world. On a bridge across the Tiber [an Italian river running through Rome] young [Roman hero] Horatius delayed briefly the advance of a superior force. Still farther back is the action of [Spartan king] Leonidas against the Persian host at the hot gates of Thermopylae [famous battle between Greeks and Persians]. The terrain and the odds were not, after all, far different from those of Robert Jordan. There is even the prediction, comparable to Pilar's, that Leonidas will die, and there is a lone Persian cavalryman who comes, like the fascist horseman in Hemingway, to reconnoitre the mountain pass. Jordan could never complain with [Anglo-American poet T.S.] Eliot's Gerontion that he had not fought at "the hot gates." His bridge is at the center of the history of holding actions; and although his problem is small in scale, it is so conceived and projected as to suggest a struggle of epical dimensions.

Epic Technique

In making such a claim for Hemingway's novel, one must reckon with his own assertion that "all bad writers are in love with the epic." Even a few gifted writers have fallen into the error of attempting too much or going about it in the wrong way. The conscious striving for an epic magnitude, as in some of [American poet Walt] Whitman's poetry and much of [American novelist Thomas] Wolfe's prose, may reduce the writing to rhetoric and enlarge the people to set-piece characters whose resemblance to human beings is merely coincidental. There is also the danger that the struggle for the cosmic may backslide into the comic. The grand manner too easily inflates to the grandiose; good sense may be sacrificed to size; quantity may be mistaken for quality; and what was meant to be great will become simply gross.

As a prose epic of the Spanish people, *For Whom the Bell Tolls* commits none of these errors. Indeed the novel is a living example of how, in modern times, the epic quality must probably be projected. The failure of certain modern practitioners of the epic manner rests perhaps primarily upon ignorance of the uses of synecdoche, the device by which a part can be made to function for the whole, and the fact to gain an emblematic power without the loss of its native particularity. Hemingway's war novel, rich as it is in symbolic extensions, is somewhere near a synecdochist's triumph.

What elements of the epic manner may be successfully adapted to modern needs? Despite the obvious gap between Spain and Ilium, the student of the epic may find part of his answer in considering the Homeric parallel [to the Greek epic poet Homer's *Iliad*]. A primitive setting, simple food and wine, the care and use of weapons, the sense of imminent danger, the emphasis on masculine prowess, the presence of varying degrees of courage and cowardice, the rude barbarisms on both sides, the operation of certain religious and magical superstitions, the warrior codes—these, surely, are common ties between the two sets of protagonists. Jordan is not to be scorned as the type of [the Greek warrior-hero] Achilles, and one can recognize in Pablo the rude outlines of a debased and sulking [Greek warrior] Ajax. Pilar the gypsy, though she reads the lifeline in Jordan's palm instead of consulting the shape and color of animal entrails, makes the consciousness of the supernatural an operative factor.

Epic Language

Nor should the technical comparisons be overlooked. One of the most interesting of these is the intentionally heightened language. [Literary critic] Mr. Edward Fenimore has published a valuable essay on the subject ["English and Spanish in *For Whom the Bell Tolls*"]. He remarks, for instance, on "the Elizabethan [sixteenth-century English] tone" of a number of phrases and sentences.

"That such a tone should haunt Hemingway's pages is [he goes on] inevitable. His tale has much of the epic in its breadth, in the plain fact that his characters mean more than themselves alone, the action they are engaged upon [being] unmistakably a culminating point pushed up by profound national or . . . universal forces. In the Elizabethan, the English possesses an epic language, and it is into the forms of this language that Hemingway, through the very nature of the world he is creating . . . constantly passes."

Yet, as Fenimore observes, this language is carefully tempered. A purely colloquial modern English and an English which belongs in its essence to the King James version of the Bible [published in 1611] are brought together to mutual advantage. One example is a brief interchange between the rough-spoken Agustín and the supremely dignified Fernando—who is, incidentally, one of Hemingway's best-drawn minor characters.

"Where the hell are you going?" Agustín asked the grave little man as he came up.

"To my duty," Fernando said with dignity.

"Thy duty," said Agustín mockingly. "I besmirch the milk of thy duty. . . ."

Several of Hemingway's short stories had made a similar collocation of the old and dignified with the new and crass. In [Hemingway's short story] "The Gambler, The Nun, and The Radio," for example, the contrast is used to underscore the humor of character. Now, however, with his temperamental sensitivity to the tone of language, and an intuitive feel for what would constitute the proper blend of ancient and modern idiom in the conduct of key scenes, whether they were comic or not, Hemingway developed a language suitable to his epic purposes. The masculine vigor in the march of the narrative comes about, not alone from the author's skill in the unfolding of events but also through his responsiveness to language values.

Outside the technical aspects of language one finds an over-all seriousness of conception which, though high enough to meet even [English poet Matthew] Arnold's stringent requirements [for good literature], does not preclude rough humor and soldierly badinage [banter]. As a means of giving depth to his characterizations, Homer knew and used (if indeed he did not invent) the device of the flashback. As for synecdoche, Homer was very far from limiting his range of significance by carefully centering his attention on the action before Troy. All bad writers may love the epic. A few good ones, working somewhat after the fashion of Hemingway, can succeed in keeping the epic genre in a state of good health by adapting transferable elements to the needs and expectations of the modern reader.

Maria Is a Victim of War

Charles J. Nolan Jr.

Charles J. Nolan Jr. is a professor of English at the US Naval Academy. He is the author of Aaron Burr and the American Literary Imagination *as well as numerous essays on the fiction of Ernest Hemingway.*

Nolan suggests in the following article that in the past scholars have pigeonholed Hemingway's women characters into stereotypical roles. However, Nolan argues, viewing female characters such as Maria in For Whom the Bell Tolls *through the lens of psychology makes them more realistic and less two-dimensional. Maria, who has been brutalized by various enemy factions, suffers greatly during the Spanish civil conflict. Nolan believes that she is clearly suffering from post-traumatic stress disorder as a result of having witnessed the death of her parents and having been raped and jailed. Nolan sites information from the* Diagnostic and Statistical Manual of Mental Disorders *(DSM) to validate his contention about Maria's emotional illness. Understanding her condition allows the reader to sympathize with her plight and her struggle to overcome her damaged emotional state.*

In 1952, Philip Young, reading [then recently deceased Austrian psychoanalyst] Otto Fenichel's *Psychoanalytic Theory of Neurosis*, suggested that [Hemingway hero] Nick Adams suffered from traumatic neurosis, and, more recently, [critic] Ronald Smith updated that diagnosis to what today we call post-traumatic stress disorder (PTSD). Neither Young nor Smith was or is a psychologist, but both help us understand

Charles J. Nolan Jr., "'A Little Crazy': Psychiatric Diagnoses of Three Hemingway Women Characters," *Hemingway Review*, vol. 28, no.2, Spring 2009, pp. 105–18. Copyright © 2009 by the Hemingway Review. All rights reserved. Reproduced by permission.

that first Hemingway hero and, by extension, all of the rest of them. Hemingway's major women characters, however, although much has been written about them, have not been examined in such a strictly psychological way. Until the 1980s, Catherine Barkley [of *A Farewell to Arms*], Brett Ashley [of *The Sun Also Rises*], and Maria were seen as either destroyers of men or fantasy figures—"bitches or goddesses"—but a later generation of scholars has worked hard to move them from stereotypes to complex women characters worthy of our attention. Still, the possibility that these women suffer from diagnosable psychological ailments has not received the kind of attention given to Nick Adams's all-too-clear symptoms. . . .

Wartime Atrocities

In some ways, Maria in *For Whom the Bell Tolls* is the easiest of the three Hemingway women to diagnose. Both a witness to wartime atrocities and a rape victim, she suffers from posttraumatic stress disorder. She watches in horror as the Guardia Civil [state security forces] execute her parents: "I saw both of them shot," she tells Robert Jordan, "and my father said, '*Viva la Republica*,' when they shot him standing against the wall of the slaughterhouse of our village." In the same way, her mother, who is killed next, cries out, "Viva my husband who was Mayor of this village." Like others who see their relatives killed, Maria is emotionally "numb": "I myself could not cry," she remembers, and she does not "notice anything that passed" as she is marched into the town square because the scene she has just witnessed keeps recurring in her mind: "I could only see my father and my mother at the moment of the shooting . . . , and this was in my head like a scream that would not die but kept on and on." The Falangists [party that supported the Fascists] then take over from the Guardia Civil and move all the women to the barbershop, where they suffer further atrocities.

Because Maria is the mayor's daughter, she is taken in first. As she watches in the mirror, hardly able to recognize her own face "because grief had changed it" and unable to feel anything, the barber cuts off her braids, strikes her repeatedly across her face with them, and uses them to gag her. Next he brands her as a Communist by using iodine to write U.H.P. (*Unión de Hermanos Proletarios* [Union of Proletarian Brothers]) on her forehead as she sits looking at him, emotionally paralyzed: "my heart was frozen in me for my father and my mother." From the barbershop the Falangists take her back to her father's office in the city hall, where she is repeatedly raped: "it was there that the bad things were done." She tells Robert, "Never did I submit to any one. Always I fought and always it took two of them or more to do me harm. One would sit on my head and hold me." Afterwards, she notes, she "wished to die."

Fragile Emotional Health

Eventually, Maria is sent to prison in [the city of] Valladolid, where prison guards shaved her head "regularly," but she is rescued by Pablo and his band when they blow up a train on which she and other prisoners are being taken south. She tells Robert that she was "somewhat crazy" at the time; according to Rafael "she would not speak and she cried all the time and if any one touched her she would shiver like a wet dog." Pilar confirms Maria's tenuous psychological state when she explores with Robert the possibility that he will take the girl with him when he leaves. The older woman does not want to have to deal with Maria again if she relapses as a result of his leaving: "I have had her crazy before and I have enough without that." Even though Maria seems to have recovered because of Pilar's care and because of her new love for Robert—"It is as though it had never happened since we were first together"—she is still fragile. She does not want to hear, for ex-

A scene from the 1943 film adaptation of For Whom the Bell Tolls. *Ingrid Bergman plays Maria (third from right).* © Paramount/The Kobal Collection.

ample, how the Fascists retook Pablo's town. Pilar's tale of the brutality that occurred when Pablo initially seized the town has already been too painful for her: "Do not tell me about it [the Fascists' re-emergence]. . . . I do not want to hear it. This [Pablo's viciousness] is enough. This was too much." Pilar agrees, noting that the story would be "bad for Maria." In fact, Maria pleads with Pilar not to tell the story to Robert either because if she is there she "might listen in spite of [her]self." When Pilar remarks that she will tell Robert when Maria is working, she is so upset that she cries out, "No. No. Please. Let us not tell it at all." "Are there no pleasant things to speak of?" she asks. "Do we have to talk always of horrors?" Even though Rafael notes that "Lately she has been much better" and Jordan himself thinks, "Maria was sound enough now," her recovery is so recent that no one wants to risk her emotional health.

Post-Traumatic Stress Disorder

There seems little question that Maria suffers from post-traumatic stress disorder (PTSD) and is gradually recovering. The traumatic events defining PTSD must involve "actual or threatened death or serious injury, or a threat to the physical integrity of self or others" [according to the *Diagnostic and Statistical Manual of Mental Disorders* (DSM)] and witnessing her parents' shooting, being brutalized in the barbershop, and then being gang-raped certainly meet the criteria. Her response of "intense fear, helplessness, or horror" is reflected by her initial emotional paralysis and her difficulty recognizing herself in the mirror. The persistent re-experiencing of the traumatic events, a clear marker of PTSD, is reflected in the scream that goes "on and on" in her head after her parents' shooting. We suspect from what she says to Robert about Pilar's advice to tell him about the sexual assault "if [she] ever began to think of it again" that she has gone over and over her ghastly ordeal in a finally (but tenuously) successful attempt to master it. In those suffering from PTSD, there is also [according to the DSM] "persistent avoidance of stimuli associated with the trauma and numbing of general responsiveness", both of which Maria exhibits. Her pleading with Pilar not to tell the story of the Fascists' retaking the town and her unwillingness to discuss with Robert the "bad things" she experienced in her father's office reflect her efforts to avoid memories of her brutalization. Her description of her "heart" as "frozen" within her for her father and her mother and her emotional detachment from her humiliation in the barber's chair are clear indications of the numbness that marks this disorder.

Maria also suffers from the "persistent symptoms of increased arousal" that PTSD victims experience, in this case an "exaggerated startle response." Rafael makes this point when he tells Robert what Maria was like after the band rescued her—she shivered whenever she was touched. In addition, her inability to speak—she is mute—and her continual crying reveal that she also has "clinically significant distress or impairment in social, occupational, or other important areas of functioning." Because she tells Robert that she has been with Pablo's band for three months and because she has been in prison in Valladolid before that for some undisclosed time, she also meets the duration criterion—symptoms still occurring "more than 1 month" after the traumatic event—for the disorder. By the novel's conclusion, however, she has apparently recovered, although there may be some lingering aftereffects.

Hemingway's Insights into His Characters

An analysis of these three "crazy" Hemingway women reveals so much about them and about their creator. Certainly, we come away with a renewed sense of the struggle they undergo as they try to live in a world that has gone to smash. Catherine's depression, Brett's borderline issues, and Maria's trauma make us sympathetic to their plights and respectful of the challenges each of them must overcome to have any chance at happiness. Although events overtake these women, we are reminded anew of just how hard the modern world is for them—and for us. About Hemingway, we recognize once more what an astute reader of human psychology he was, drawing insights both from his own interior struggles and from observations of those suffering around him. There is much to be learned from great writers, especially about the inner life that has such power to shape behavior and such importance in understanding others. Hemingway has taught us a lot with these three damaged but vital characters.

Social Issues in Literature

CHAPTER 3

Contemporary Perspectives on War

The Afghanistan War Must Be Won

The Economist

The Economist is an international newspaper based in London, England, that covers weekly news and world affairs.

The following viewpoint from the British newspaper The Economist *argues that, despite the costliness and longevity of the Afghanistan War, America and Great Britain must stay the course. The war has taken its toll on both countries as well as its allies, including Canada and the Netherlands, that are involved in the fighting, but the cost of losing the war could be much greater. Great Britain should act with conviction and throw more of its support, in troops and supplies, to the war. Although the Afghan conflict has been raging for years, the push to pacify Afghanistan is just beginning. This is a war that must be won.*

It has been a bloody month [in July 2009] in Afghanistan but America's allies, especially Britain, should not lose heart.

Afghanistan is said to be the graveyard of empires. The British army came to grief there in the 19th century, the Soviet one in the 20th. Such was Afghans' reputation for ferocity that [nineteenth-century British novelist] Rudyard Kipling told those left wounded on Afghanistan's plains: "Jest roll to your rifle and blow out your brains." These days British soldiers are again dying in Afghanistan, along with Americans, Canadians and many others. The Taliban [Islamic militant and political group] are resurgent. Each fighting season is bloodier than the last.

Agonizing over the War

President Barack Obama is deploying an extra 20,000 troops there this year [in 2009]. But some allies are already on their way out. The Netherlands will withdraw fighting forces next year, followed by Canada in 2011. Now the public in Britain, which has the second-largest contingent in Afghanistan, is agonising over the country's role in the war after a dreadful month in Helmand [Province in Afghanistan].

After eight years of disheartening warfare, it is tempting to see NATO's [North Atlantic Treaty Organization's] mission as a repeat of past misadventures in the Hindu Kush [mountain range in Afghanistan]. The Soviets lost even though they had more troops than NATO has today, a more powerful Afghan army and were supported by a cadre of motivated Afghan communists. But such comparisons are wrong. Unlike the anti-Soviet mujahideen [Islamic warriors], who were backed by America, Saudi Arabia and Pakistan, the Taliban have no superpower sponsor. In the 1980s Soviet aircraft were shot down with American-made Stinger missiles; today NATO has mastery of the skies. The Taliban are a Pushtun [an ethnic group in Afghanistan] faction, not a national movement; their insurgency is largely limited to the southern half of the country.

Afghans may feel anger over the death of civilians killed by foreign forces, frustration at the chaos and insecurity, and dismay at the corruption of [Afghan] President Hamid Karzai's government. But opinion polls say that most want Western troops to stay; they remember the misery of the civil war and the oppression of Taliban rule too well. They want the West to do a better job of securing the country.

A Costly War

For America Afghanistan is a war of necessity; it is from there that [Islamic militant leader] Osama bin Laden ordered the attacks of September 11th, 2001. For many European allies, though, it is less vital—a war of solidarity with America, a war of choice. Such operations quickly turn unpopular when they go badly, and governments tend to inflate their aims. Gordon Brown, the British prime minister, talks of promoting "an emerging democracy".

Critics say the effort is misconceived: the real danger is in Pakistan, where al-Qaeda's [Islamist organization responsible for the 9/11 attacks, among others] leaders are now hiding. But helping Pakistan fight Islamic militants will only be harder if the Taliban and al-Qaeda can claim victory in Afghanistan. Others say the West is being over-ambitious. It can never hope to create a stable democracy in Afghanistan; all it needs is a small contingent to protect Kabul [the Afghan capital] and some special forces and bombers to deal with any returning al-Qaeda fighters. But such a minimalist approach is what allowed the Taliban to regroup.

The cost to NATO countries is immediately apparent: tens of billions of dollars and the lives of more than 1,200 soldiers. The cost of leaving is harder to measure but is probably larger: the return of the Taliban to power; an Afghan civil war; the utter destabilisation of nuclear-armed Pakistan; the restoration of al-Qaeda's Afghan haven; the emboldening of every jihadist [Islamic militant fighting what he perceives to be a holy war against the infidels] in the world; and the weakening of the West's friends.

Friends and Allies

Britain's ambition to be a global "force for good" comes at a cost. As America's best friend, with privileged access to intelligence, it feels compelled to take part in America's wars. As the most capable militarily of NATO's European members (together with France), it helps to rally others. But fighting in Afghanistan is not just about prestige. With its large population of Pakistani origin, it has much at stake in helping to maintain the stability of Afghanistan and Pakistan. London has been attacked by al-Qaeda more recently than New York.

So what should Britain do? To begin with, the government must act with conviction, rather than wish the problem away. It cannot be at war with a peacetime mind-set. As a share of the budget, defence spending has shrunk since 2001. The defence ministry is a parking place for weak ministers or a stepping-stone for strong ones. Priority should be given to manning fully the army's ranks, and probably expanding them. More must be done to provide helicopters, transport aircraft, drones and better-protected vehicles. This would wreck budgets and upset the navy and air force. So be it. Losing a war is even more demoralising than losing ships or jets. The government should have announced a Strategic Defence Review a long time ago, not delayed it until after the election.

At the very least Mr. Brown should agree to the army's request for a permanent uplift of 2,000 troops for Helmand. Western forces are never going to garrison the whole province, let alone Afghanistan. But what they hold must be held securely. And above all, they must train and expand the Afghan army and police so they can gradually take over. That will not be cheap, but it is the best way to bring home Western troops.

Just the Beginning

In many ways, the push to pacify Afghanistan is only just starting, now that the war in Iraq is ending. America's marines launched a big operation in Helmand on July 2nd [2009]. Afghanistan's presidential elections take place next month. It will not be clear until the autumn, and probably not until late next year, whether Mr Obama's "surge" [troop expansion] has worked.

This is not the time to lose heart. Security must be improved, economic activity encouraged, government strengthened and insurgents offered inducements to defect. But for those things to happen, the Taliban must see that the Afghan government and its foreign friends are winning, not losing.

The Media Fueled the Run-Up to the Iraq War

Matthew Rothschild

Matthew Rothschild is the editor of the Progressive *magazine. He has appeared on* Nightline, The O'Reilly Factor, C-SPAN, *and National Public Radio (NPR), and his newspaper commentaries have run in the* Chicago Tribune, *the* Los Angeles Times, *the* Miami Herald, *and other newspapers. He is the author of* You Have No Rights: Stories of America in an Age of Repression.

Rothschild cites recognized media personalities who admit that the mainstream media was less than objective about the US rationale for attacking Iraq. In the patriotic fervor that followed the terrorist attacks of 9/11/2001, the media themselves were loath to oppose the George W. Bush administration's plans to declare war on Saddam Hussein. Moreover, Rothschild writes, key members of the media admitted that they did not perform their jobs as objective reporters, but instead allowed themselves to be pressured by the Bush administration and their own corporate executives. Prior to the war, Rothschild demonstrates, the Bush administration unleashed on the media a hoard of analysts who supported the war, while antiwar voices were barely heard. Until the mainstream media does its job properly, Rothschild argues, the American public is subject to manipulation by its own government.

An amazing thing happened on [newsman] Anderson Cooper's CNN program on May 28 [2008]. He was rehashing the Scott McClellan story [George W. Bush's former

Matthew Rothschild, "Mainstream Media Culpability," *The Progressive*, vol. 8, no. 7, July 2008, p. 8.

press secretary who accused the administration of deceptive practices] when CNN's [reporter] Jessica Yellin began to make a startling confession of her own, which to my mind was just as newsworthy as McClellan's.

Enormous Pressure

Here's what she said:

"The press corps was under enormous pressure from corporate executives, frankly, to make sure that this was a war presented in a way that was consistent with the patriotic fever in the nation and the President's high approval ratings," she said.

She added: "The higher the President's approval ratings, the more pressure I had from news executives—and I wasn't at this network at the time—to put on positive stories about the President." Anderson Cooper seemed surprised at this, and asked a follow-up. Yellin answered: "They would turn down stories that were more critical, and try to put on pieces that were more positive."

The next day she wrote on her CNN blog that she was referring to her time at [cable news network] MSNBC. She tried to backpedal a little, but she didn't deny it all.

"No senior corporate leadership ever asked me to take out a line in a script or rewrite an anchor intro," she wrote. "I did not mean to leave the impression that corporate executives were interfering in my daily work; my interaction was with senior producers. What was clear to me is that many people running the broadcasts wanted coverage that was consistent with the patriotic fever in the country at the time. It was clear to me they wanted their coverage to reflect the mood of the country."

MSNBC had made that clear to [liberal talk show host] Phil Donahue, as well, when it canceled his show in the lead-up to the Iraq War. One internal memo said Donahue's show presented a "difficult public face for NBC [which partners with Microsoft in MSNBC] in a time of war. . . . He seems to delight in presenting guests who are anti-war, anti-Bush, and skeptical of the Administration's motives." This was not good, the memo said, at a time when "our competitors are waving the flag at every opportunity." Now McClellan, of all people, rises to reproach this kind of media performance, acting like some improbable journalism professor.

Patriotism Run Amok

"We in the Bush Administration had no difficulty in getting our messages out to the American people," McClellan writes in *What Happened. Inside the Bush White House and Washington's Culture of Deception.* "If anything, the national press corps was probably too deferential to the White House and to the Administration in regard to the most important decision facing the nation during my years in Washington, the choice over whether to go to war in Iraq. The collapse of the Administration's rationales for war, which became apparent months after our invasion, should never have come as such a surprise. The public should have been made much more aware, before the fact, of the uncertainties, doubts, and caveats that underlay the intelligence about the regime of [Iraqi dictator] Saddam Hussein."

After the McClellan-Yellin confessions came tumbling out, network news anchors weighed in, and only CBS's [newscaster and talk show host] Katie Couric copped to the charge. Speaking on *The Early Show* on CBS, Couric said it was "one of the most embarrassing chapters in American journalism." She acknowledged pressure from "the corporations who own where we work and from the government itself to really squash any kind of dissent or any kind of questioning of it." At the time, Couric was a host of the NBC *Today* show.

Yellin's and Couric's revelations dovetail with similar ones made several years ago by CNN's [reporter] Christiane Amanpour and CBS's [network news anchor] Dan Rather.

In September 2003, in response to a question from [journalist] Tina Brown on CNBC about whether the media "drank the Kool Aid" [i.e., unquestioningly accepted, in reference to the 1978 incident where members of the Reverend Jim Jones's People's Temple followed his lead in committing mass suicide by drinking cyanide-laced Kool-Aid] on Iraq, Amanpour responded: "I think the press was muzzled, and I think the press self-muzzled. I'm sorry to say, but certainly television—and, perhaps, to a certain extent, my station—was intimidated by the Administration and its foot soldiers at Fox News. And it did, in fact, put a climate of fear and self-censorship, in my view, in terms of the kind of broadcast work we did." She added that journalists "did not ask enough questions, for instance, about weapons of mass destruction. I mean, it looks like this was disinformation at the highest levels."

And a couple of years before he was cashiered [fired], Dan Rather said the media engaged in "self-censorship" after 9/11.

"In some ways the fear is that you will be necklaced here, you will have a flaming tire of lack of patriotism put around your neck," he told the BBC [British Broadcasting Corporation]. "Now it is that fear that keeps journalists from asking the toughest of the tough questions. . . . What we are talking about here—whether one wants to recognize it or not, or call it by its proper name or not—is a form of self-censorship. It starts with a feeling of patriotism within oneself. It carries through with a certain knowledge that the country as a whole—and for all the right reasons—felt and continues to feel this surge of patriotism within themselves. And one finds oneself saying: 'I know the right question, but you know what? This is not exactly the right time to ask it.'"

Rather termed this phenomenon "patriotism run amok."

The mainstream media has not come anywhere close to a proper self-examination of its role in peddling the propaganda of the Bush Administration. Whether it was a half-hearted apology from *The New York Times* for the lies of Judith Miller

[*New York Times* journalist who erroneously reported on weapons of mass distruction in Iraq] that it put on its front page several times or a faint mea culpa ["my fault"] from Howard Kurtz of *The Washington Post* [who wrote a piece admitting serious mistakes in *The Washington Post's* pre-war coverage of weapons of mass destruction in the Iraq], the print media have not fully accounted for their role as the handmaidens of the Iraq War.

The Media Must Do Its Job

The networks have been even more remiss.

Let's look at the record.

In the three-week period surrounding [then secretary of state] Colin Powell's address to the United Nations on February 5, 2003, there were 393 sources who appeared on the three leading network news shows, as well as PBS's [Public Broadcasting System] *NewsHour with Jim Lehrer*. Only 6 percent were skeptical of the need for war, and only three (less than 1 percent) were anti-war activists, according to a study by the great media watchdog group Fairness and Accuracy in Reporting. More than three-quarters of the sources were current or former government officials.

In April, *The New York Times* revealed how the Pentagon in 2005 put together a group of more than seventy-five retired military officers, many of them engaged with private defense contractors, to front for the Pentagon on TV and radio. The networks typically did not disclose the connections—or the coaching from the Pentagon handlers. Inside the Pentagon, these military analysts were referred to as "message force multipliers" or "surrogates," the *Times* story said. They had extraordinary access, meeting personally with then-Defense Secretary Donald Rumsfeld at least eighteen times.

At one meeting, one of the analysts called the briefings "Psyops"—psychological operations.

"What are you, some kind of a nut?" Rumsfeld responded sarcastically, eliciting laughter, the *Times* noted. "You don't believe in the Constitution?" These military analysts made 4,500 appearances, according to Media Matters for America. They popped up on ABC, CBS, CNBC, CNN, Fox, MSNBC, NBC, and NPR [National Public Radio]. Surprise, surprise, the networks downplayed this story.

Some of the shady practices of the mainstream media continue. I've just seen a new report by ABC News with the title, "Iran in Secret Talks with Al Qaeda [the militant Islamic group responsible for the attacks on 9/11, among others], U.S. Officials Say." The story itself isn't as alarming as the headline, since it deals with Al Qaeda operatives that Iran has held under arrest since 2003. Like many of the erroneous stories in the mainstream media leading up to the Iraq War, this one relies on unnamed sources. The story, by Jonathan Karl, does not cite a single official by name. Instead, eleven times it refers to a "U.S. official" or a "senior U.S. official" or a "senior defense official" or a "high-ranking U.S. military officer."

The Bush Administration, Scott McClellan, and the mainstream media all sold America a bill of goods—a very costly bill of goods at that. Until the mainstream media starts doing its job, the public and our democracy will remain vulnerable to the manipulators in the White House.

The Spanish Civil War Offers Important Lessons About the Iraq War

Stephen Schwartz

Stephen Schwartz writes for the conservative periodical the The Weekly Standard. *He is coauthor of* Spanish Marxism vs. Soviet Communism: A History of the POUM.

In the following viewpoint, written during the Iraq War, Schwartz argues that there are significant similarities between the Spanish Civil War and the conflict in Iraq. Schwartz notes that the Spanish Civil War, in pitting the Loyalists against the Fascists, served as a precursor to World War II. Both Nazi Germany and Fascist Italy aided the fight against the Spanish republic. He quotes British leaders who say that their country should have intervened in Spain in the thirties and that doing so might have slowed the Nazi juggernaut. Schwartz draws parallels with the current Middle East, where the United States and Great Britain received little help from other countries in fighting for democracy in Iraq. Winning in Iraq, Schwartz argues, might save the world from an even greater future conflict.

Joseph Lieberman, Democratic senator from Connecticut and independent candidate for a new term [in 2006], shared a remarkable insight in Hartford on August 22 [2006]. He commented ..., "Iraq, if you look back at it, is going to be like the Spanish Civil War, which was the harbinger of what was to come."

Useful Lessons

The Spanish strife of 1936–39 remains, seventy years after it began, one of the central incidents of the century we lately left behind. And it offers numerous precedents for the global war on terror.

Lieberman probably intended to express little more than the standard informed opinion on Spain's war—that the Western democracies made the Second World War inevitable by failing to save the Spanish Republic from rightist dictator Gen. Francisco Franco, who was a proxy for [German dictator Adolf] Hitler and [Italian dictator Benito] Mussolini.

The aptness of the Spain-Iraq parallel has struck others. The same day as Lieberman made his comment, a British paper, the Citizen, editorialized: "[T]he Spanish Civil War, besides presaging the Second World War, had important repercussions. . . . [T]hose who question what has happened today in recent zones of conflict, especially Israel-Lebanon, could do no better than undertake a revisitation of history which could teach all of us some useful lessons about the threats of fascism, totalitarianism and religious extremism." [English] Labour member of the House of Commons Denis MacShane, who happens to be the biographer of former Tory prime minister Edward Heath, recently argued that Britain should have intervened in Spain on the side of the republic and noted that Heath held the same view.

Similarly, on August 18, [the Washington conservative think tank] Heritage Foundation analyst Ariel Cohen, writing in the *Washington Times*, compared pro-Hezbollah [terrorist group] demonstrators in Washington to the "Fifth Column . . . the pro-fascist forces in Republican Madrid during the Spanish Civil War of the 1930s. Today's Fifth Column glorifies the global jihad [Islamic holy war] against the West." And a few days before that, radical Islam expert Daniel Pipes, on the Lou Dobbs show, likened the Hezbollah-Israel war to "the Spanish Civil War as a precursor to World War II."

The argument is a powerful and correct one, although it has its subtleties and flaws. First, Iraq is not now in a state of civil war. Wide-scale, continuous combat between major internal forces has not started in Iraq. And it may not, thanks to the overwhelming demographic weight of the Shia Muslims, a majority of whom are committed to the new Iraqi state.

But the analogy with the Spanish Civil War does not depend on the existence of an unrestrained military struggle between Iraqi factions. The Spain-Iraq parallel contains a deeper lesson for the present. The Spanish Civil War was the first major example of the modern phenomenon of proxy wars, in which local clashes are exploited, and third countries torn apart, in the competition between regional and global alliances. Spain was not a simple war of conquest and pillage, like the contemporaneous Japanese invasion of China and Italian assault on Ethiopia. Rather, Spain represented a confrontation between the politics of the past, represented by Franco, and the politics of the future, embodied in a confused but nonetheless genuine Republic.

Spain and Iraq

Franco was not a true fascist—his system had very few of the sociological or ideological characteristics of Mussolini's and Hitler's party-states. Rather, Franco was a soldier bent on preventing a social revolution by means of a coup. Nevertheless, the Franco cause was profoundly identified with fascism, because Germany lent the Spanish general the best elements of the Nazi air force, and Italy sent thousands of soldiers to fight alongside Franco's troops. But neither was the Spanish Republican cause stainless. It was the victim of subversion by its alleged ally, the Soviet Union, and many of its strongest supporters considered democracy a bourgeois fraud.

Yet the historical dynamics of internal discord and international engagement show a persistent pattern from then to now. Spain, like Iraq, was a country without a firm national

General Francisco Franco led Fascist forces in a coup against the Spanish Republic during the Spanish Civil War. Here Franco monitors the action at the front through binoculars in 1936. © UK History/Alamy.

identity. In Spain, the Castilian [from the state of Castile] aristocracy controlled the state, most of the tax income, the army, and the Catholic Church—the latter an ideological pillar of the old order. As if cast from an identical historical mold, Iraq long suffered under the corrupt and brutal rule of the Sunni elite, which used its clerical wing to help maintain its power.

Spanish entrepreneurship and economic development were most advanced in the Basque [in northern Spain] and Catalan [in northeastern Spain] regions, whose cultural affiliations with the Madrid monarchy were weakened. In corresponding fashion, the Iraqi Kurds have leaped far ahead in modernization, yet like the Basques and Catalans, they are culturally and linguistically distinct from, and resentful of, the Iraqi Arabs.

Spain in 1936 included a vast and turbulent mass of radical industrial workers and farm laborers whose political culture was mainly anarchist, and whose aspirations were barely perceived, much less understood, in the outside world. Iraq's Shia majority resembles the Spanish anarchists—there are many of them, they are militant, and they often seem to have no friends. So the Iraqi Shias, like the Spanish left, are enticed into a dangerous courtship with a totalitarian suitor: Iran plays the role in Basra [Iraq] that Russian Stalinism [the ideology of Soviet leader Joseph Stalin] had in Barcelona [Spain].

Spain at war, like Iraq, became an arena for massacres and militias, hostage-taking and disappearances, assassinations and reprisals. The Franco forces murdered the poet Federico Garcia Lorca; Soviet agents who infiltrated the Republican police killed a dissident Catalan Marxist author, Andreu Nin. The competing ideologies in Spain also included Carlism, an extreme form of monarchism [supporters of royalty], as well as anarchism [which opposes state governments], no less volatile than the cruel doctrines of Wahhabism [a reactionary movement within Sunni Islam], the inspirer of the late [Jordanian militant] Abu Musab al Zarqawi, and the Shia extremism of [Iraqi political leader] Moktada al-Sadr. And as Germany and Italy helped Franco, so elements in Saudi Arabia finance and recruit Sunni terrorists to kill in Iraq, while Iran supports Iraqi Shia paramilitary expansion.

These correlates are not limited to the Spanish and Iraqi hostilities—they apply to the main historical chapters since Spain. The Spanish war anticipated Communist-run civil wars during the late 1940s, in Greece and in various Asian countries including China, India, Burma, Korea, Malaysia, the Philippines, and, of course, Indochina [i.e., Vietnam, Cambodia, and Laos]. The pattern continued through Central America and Africa in the last years of the Soviet empire. The Spanish war had its most dramatic repetition, until now, in the former Yugoslavia. Think of the Serbs as equivalent to Castilians in Spain and Sunnis in Iraq, and the original motif reappears.

Preventing a More Terrible War

But the main points of resemblance between Spain and Iraq—and even Lebanon under the menace of Hezbollah—remain the role of the international powers, the great contention between oppression and liberation, and the threat of a later, wider war. When France, which had a leftist government in the late '30s, and Britain, which should have served as a sentinel against Nazi interference beyond Germany's borders, together accepted an embargo on arms to the Spanish Republic, Hitler was encouraged beyond measure in his plans for the subjugation of all Europe. These days, the pusillanimity [cowardliness] of European leaders allows Hassan Nasrallah, the Hezbollah chief, to threaten the complete destruction of the nascent Lebanese democracy while also attacking the citizens of northern Israel.

In Iraq, unlike in Spain, the United States, almost alone but for Britain, has undertaken the heavy task of leading the world's democratic faithful against the acolytes of terror, who are now driven by Islamofascism [militant Islamic groups] rather than its antecedents, the antidemocratic ideologies of the 1930s. That is the ultimate lesson of Spain in 1936 and Iraq in 2006: By winning the battle of Iraq, and by fostering real change in Saudi Arabia, Syria, and Iran, the democratic nations may save the world from a later, longer, bloodier, and more terrible war.

In the Spanish Civil War, [French writer] Albert Camus wrote, he and those like him "learned that one can be right and be beaten." Let us hope that, so many decades later, Sen. Lieberman and those like him are not alone in this understanding: that we are right, and that we will not be beaten.

America Failed to Accomplish Its Goals in Iraq

Jed Babbin

Jed Babbin served as a deputy undersecretary of defense in the George H.W. Bush administration. He is a contributing editor for the The American Spectator and writes the Loose Canons column for its online edition.

Babbin argues in the following viewpoint that, while the debate over the Iraq War continues, it is clear that America did not accomplish what it set out to do. After the initial US victory, Babbin states, two competing plans were put forth by the United States. One was to set up a provisional Iraqi government and withdraw. The second, which ultimately prevailed, was to engage in nation building. But Islamic militants had other ideas, according to Babbin. They flooded into Iraq, determined to disrupt the postwar process, and they largely succeeded until General David Petraeus ordered the now-famous surge in American troops. But Iraq and Afghanistan are not candidates for democracy, Babbin argues, and the repercussions of the American troop withdrawal remain to be seen.

Historians may someday conclude that the most curious incident of Barack Obama's presidency occurred in October 2011. When Obama announced that the last of our troops would be withdrawn from Iraq by year's end, the news was almost lost amid the tsunami of economic news and metronomic [mechanically regular] campaign debates. There were no great outpourings of emotion, ringing speeches, or UN hy-

Jed Babbin, "Iraq in the Rearview Mirror," *The American Spectator*, vol. 44, no. 10, December 2011, p. 68.

perbole. The moment was, like [fictional British detective] Sherlock Holmes' observation of the dog in the night-time, curious because of the silence that surrounded it.

A Costly and Ineffective War

Why would the most controversial war since Vietnam end without as much controversy as when it began? The reason is that America tuned out the Iraq war years ago. The horrific Sunni vs. Shia [two branches of Islam] violence that overwhelmed Iraq after the Samarra mosque [a holy site to the Shias] bombing in February 2006 was quelled by [American] General [David] Petraeus's troop surge. When the violence subsided to Iraq's new normal, so did the controversy. From late 2008, America has been interested in almost nothing but economic news. And, from 2009, we've had a president who kept the willing media focused on everything other than the war.

Too little political attention has been paid to the war in general and Iraq in particular. To the extent that Americans debated the war at all, Iraq, Afghanistan, and Pakistan—and the deaths of [al Qaeda (Islamic militant organization responsible for 9/11 attacks) leader] Osama bin Laden and [Islamic leader] Anwar al-Awlaki—were isolated events, worlds away from the economic crisis that diverted our attention from everything else.

We know, from the memoirs of [president] George W. Bush, [vice president] Richard Cheney, [secretary of defense] Donald Rumsfeld, [British prime minister] Tony Blair, and [director of central intelligence] George Tenet, the reasons for the decision to launch the U.S. invasion of Iraq. They've also tried to explain the choice of a post-war occupation and nation-building effort that commenced there and in Afghanistan. That wisdom (or lack of it) cannot be measured at this moment in time.

Too many books have already been written on whether we "won" or "lost" the war in Iraq. That question is unresolved because of President Bush's failure—and that of his successor—to define correctly the war that began on 9/11. (There is a strong argument that it began long before 9/11, with bin Laden's fatwa [religious decree] against America in 1996, or as far back as 1979 with the advent of the Iranian kakistocracy [government by the worst citizens].) Neither Bush nor Obama had the wisdom to define it correctly as a war with the nations that sponsor terrorism and the hegemonic [dominance] ideology of Islam that propels them. That war could not have been won within the borders of Iraq, though it may have been lost.

We know what it has cost us. At this writing [December 2011], we've spent 4,287 American lives. Last summer, the Congressional Budget Office estimated the cost of the war at that date was about $709 billion. (The Congressional Research Service set the cost higher at $748 billion.)

President Bush said (and wrote in his memoir) that our goal was a unified, democratic Iraq that could govern itself, sustain itself, defend itself, and serve as an ally in the "War on Terror." As we shall see, it's apparent that no part of this goal has been achieved, and that the progress made toward them is fleeting.

American Accomplishments

So what have we accomplished in Iraq? Are these accomplishments worth the sacrifices we—or, more accurately, our military—have made? It appears that our principal accomplishment in Iraq is that we have given the Iraqi people their freedom. It is theirs to use as they see fit. Have we? And is it?

For decades before 2003, Iraq had been ruled by a Baathist [Iraqi political party] dictator who had tortured and murdered his people, sometimes en masse, even with chemical weapons. Saddam [Hussein, the just-mentioned dictator] was

Sunni, and oppressed the Shia relentlessly. Some of their most prominent clerics allied themselves with Iran, overcoming the Arab-Persian enmity solely to seek succor [relief] from Saddam's repression.

Iraqi Kurds were relatively rich, their northern homeland containing some of the nation's biggest oil fields. But their border with Turkey was often aflame with cross-border military action by Kurdish terrorists known as the PKK [Kurdistan Workers' Party] and Turkey's actions against them.

From these facts we should have understood that Iraq was not a nation. Its citizens had no unifying loyalty to an Iraqi state. They were not bound by a common purpose to a common good. Iraq and Afghanistan were nations in name only before we invaded them, and are not nations now. In neither state is there a strong nationalist spirit that overcomes tribal and religious rivalries.

We invaded Afghanistan quickly after 9/11, and chased the Taliban [the ruling political faction] out of [the capital] Kabul in short order. But it was a very shallow and inconclusive victory. President Bush, as his memoir says, believed we had a moral obligation to leave "something better" behind there than the primitive dictatorship we drove out. Unless we captured or killed bin Laden and Taliban leader Mullah Omar—both hard, elusive targets—a "victory" in Afghanistan to adequately avenge the 9/11 attacks had no tangible goal.

Over this loomed Saddam Hussein's Iraq. Since the 1991 Gulf War, Saddam had consistently defied one UN Security Council resolution after another. His military forces challenged the "no-fly zone" (enforced by U.S. and British aircraft) often, resulting in increased tension and occasional firefights when our air forces—or those of the British—fired at Iraqi anti-aircraft missile sites in response to Iraqi action targeting or actually shooting at them.

Saddam played his role to the letter, defying the U.N., playing host to some of the most notorious terrorists, such as

[Palestinian militant leader] Abu Nidal and—as we later discovered—al Qaeda's Abu Musab al-Zarqawi. The game he played—refusing to cooperate with UN weapons inspectors to conceal from his loyalists that he lacked the weapons he was thought to have—was ultimately his undoing.

American Plans vs. Terrorists' Strategies

The U.S. invasion and the defeat of Saddam's forces were a foregone conclusion, but what came afterward was not. In January 2003, President Bush was presented with two plans for post-invasion Iraq. One, authored by Defense Secretary Donald Rumsfeld and Chairman of the Joint Chiefs of Staff Gen. Richard Myers, was endorsed by the entire military community. It planned for a provisional Iraqi government to be stood up and the withdrawal of U.S. forces in a matter of months. The alternative—authored by Secretary of State Colin Powell and CIA Director George Tenet—provided for an extended occupation and another nation-building exercise.

The Rumsfeld-Myers plan would have deprived the nations that sponsor terrorism—Iran, Syria, Saudi Arabia, and the rest—of the opportunity to engage us in a long war. But just as he did in Afghanistan, Bush chose nation-building.

Between the Afghanistan invasion and the Iraq invasion, America's strategy and tactics had taught our very observant enemies much. By the fall of 2002, it was evident to all but French Foreign Minister Dominique de Villepin that an American invasion of Iraq was inevitable. From what we know now, it is apparent that in that pre-war season in 2002, the enemy made a strategic decision: to try to engage America in a long and costly insurgency in Iraq, to bleed us to death while we tried to do in Iraq what we were trying to do in Afghanistan.

In military terms, the enemy chose to make this a "meeting engagement," one on which the course of the war could be decided.

In 2002, Abu Musab al-Zarqawi entered Iraq possibly to obtain medical treatment for a wound received in Afghanistan. His "treatment" rapidly evolved into the establishment of an active al Qaeda cell in preparation for whatever America might undertake against Saddam. He was not the only terrorist to migrate to Iraq before the American invasion.

As I wrote in *The American Spectator* online on April 1, 2003, Saddam welcomed them in, mistaking the fact that they were flocking to Iraq as allegiance to him. They had no such allegiance. They came to Iraq to make Bush's goal of a unified and democratic Iraq impossible to achieve. They came, in an unsteady stream, not only from the terror-sponsoring nations but also from as far away as Ethiopia and Europe. After the invasion began, the unsteady stream became a flood. In late March 2003, about 900 members of the Ansar al-Islam group, part of bin Laden's terrorist network, were intercepted on their way into Iraq from Iran. Our forces killed about 200 and the rest fled back into Iran. By the time Saddam's regime was toppled, the insurgency was ready.

Continued Violence

Also ready and eager to help was the Shia cleric Moqtada al-Sadr. A descendant of Shia ayatollahs [Islamic leaders], al-Sadr was, in 2003, wanted on the charge of murdering Grand Ayatollah al-Khoi, a rival to his growing power. When U.S. troops got close to his stronghold in [the Iraqi city of] Najaf, the new U.S. prefect in Iraq—L. Paul "Jerry" Bremer—decided not to arrest al-Sadr. Sadr's militia was, and remains, Iran's instrument in Iraq, and a principal threat to Iraq's future.

After the invasion, Iran, Syria, and other terror sponsors made good on their plan to tie us down and make impossible Bush's goal of a democratic Iraq. Jerry Bremer made it easier for them by disbanding Saddam's army. When the Iraqi government decided to rehire most of them, the most elementary failure—the failure to pay when promised—drove many into the ranks of the insurgents.

In December 2005, while visiting Baghdad, I was briefed by a three-star Army general about the newly invented "explosively-formed penetrator [EFP]," a sophisticated land mine that compressed and propelled an extremely dense metal "bullet" to penetrate U.S. Humvees [high mobility multipurpose wheeled vehicle] and armored vehicles, killing many of our troops. The "EFP" was made exclusively in Iran. The general told me that we knew several of the places where the EFP's were being made. When I asked him why we weren't going into Iran to destroy those mini-factories, he said that our forces weren't permitted to do so.

On that same trip, visiting Marines in Camp Fallujah a day or two later, I asked the Marine commanding officer about the reports of jihadis [Islamic holy warriors] coming into Iraq from Syria, mainly through the [Iraqi] city of al-Qaim near the Syrian border. Eight months before my visit, insurgents had driven Iraqi forces out of al-Qaim. The Marine told me he had no "cross-border" problems there. The reason was that, by the time I arrived, Marine aircraft were patrolling the border hunting for jihadis. As long as the Marines were there, the insurgents weren't.

The insurgent violence peaked after the Sunni bombing of one of Shia Islam's holiest sites, the Samarra mosque, in February 2006. In 2007, General Petraeus began quelling that round of violence with his troop surge.

By then, al Qaeda had alienated many of the key Sunni chiefs in the "Sunni Triangle," and those same chiefs were willing allies as long as Petraeus left troops in their villages at night to provide security. In a July 2007 interview with the *Christian Science Monitor*, Petraeus talked about how U.S. troops had established a forward operating camp in one part of the Sunni Triangle: "This area was a very important sanctuary for al Qaeda for a number of years [since the 2003 U.S.-led invasion]. They would plan and organize car bombs and bring foreign fighters and launch them into Baghdad," Petraeus said. "We tried to disrupt [their operations] . . . but never took this away from them. That is what we're trying to do now—deny them this area." The same was true in the rest of Iraq. Where we were, violence decreased dramatically. Where we weren't, the insurgents had free rein.

Since establishing a government, the Iraqis have held more than one election in the relative security we provided. In 2005, the national election was boycotted by the Sunnis. Five years later, in March 2010, they held an election that may be the predicate to their nation's future.

The parliamentary election resulted in a split: the party of the incumbent prime minister, Nouri al-Maliki, lost by a narrow margin (89–91 seats) to former prime minister Ayad Alawi. Election day violence took at least 38 lives.

Maliki remained in office by creating a coalition with Moqtada al-Sadr's party. Though Maliki may have desired some continued U.S. presence, al-Sadr was determined to block it. Obama didn't want us to withdraw before the 2012 election, because he wanted Iraq and Afghanistan to be off the front pages while he campaigned. His representatives practically begged the Iraqis to let us stay, but the Maliki-Sadr coalition imposed conditions that even Obama couldn't accept.

Iraqi sectarian violence has been increasing since the beginning of 2011, but hasn't yet reached the levels of 2006–2007. In October, Kurdish PKK members fought a cross-border incursion by Turkish forces. Turkish Prime Minister [Recep Tayyip] Erdogan is apparently willing to increase military action in northern Iraq to defeat the Kurds and extend Turkey's power. And then there is Iran.

Iran's power over Iraq, largely exerted directly through Moqtada al-Sadr, is sufficient to control Iraq's future. Iran's interest is to keep Iraq unstable, and that is a low bar over which to leap.

Unfulfilled Goals

We have accomplished much in Iraq. Saddam is gone and a democracy of sorts is in power. Much of the nation is—for the moment—secure and Iraq's military and security forces are as well trained as they can be. But for all the good we've done in Iraq, the illusion that is Iraq remains. General Petraeus always said that our accomplishments were fragile and reversible. They are as fragile as the idea that Iraq is a nation, and they will be reversed as quickly as Iran, Turkey, and others can make them disappear.

In a televised discussion with an Iraqi parliamentarian about four years ago, I warned that Iraq could cease to be a nation after American forces withdrew. He disagreed vehemently. He said, as I recall, that the sky will always be blue, the grass will always be green, and Iraq will always be Iraq.

The gentleman was wrong and profoundly so. The Kurds could be a nation if the Turks permitted them to be, but they will not. The Sunni in central Iraq could be a part of Syria or even Saudi Arabia, if Iran permitted it, but Iran won't. And the Shia in central and southern Iraq could be absorbed by Iran, but that too would not be more permanent than the historical Arab-Persian enmity.

As we leave Iraq, its politicians and its neighbors are positioning themselves for the next round of conflict. The Shia are spreading fear that a successful revolt against Bashar al-Assad's Syrian dictatorship could be the precursor of a more aggressive Sunni Syrian attack on Iraq. It's the sort of message Iran would send, seeking a Syrian Chamberlain [like British prime minister Neville Chamberlain, who took an isolationist stance prior to World War II] to surrender some Iraqi Sudetenland [part of the former Czechoslovakia "annexed" by Hitler, an act ignored by the British and French] to them. Nouri al-Maliki's hold on power is tenuous, and Turkey's Erdogan is glancing at Kurdish terrorists and oil fields with a jaundiced eye.

For America, there is no reason to stay in Iraq any longer. We have done what we could in pursuit of Bush and Obama's wrong-headed nation-building strategy, and in that we have failed.

Nation-building is a sort of laboratory experiment, something of a board game to be taught at a foreign policy school. When we have tried it, wherever we have tried it, we have assumed that nation-building is something that can be done within a nation's borders. That was true in post-war Japan and Germany because no other nation had the power to interfere effectively. Just the opposite is true in Iraq.

Neither Iraq nor Afghanistan can be built as a democracy for two reasons. Just as Iraq is a concatenation [linkage] of neighbors without a uniting nationalism, the Afghan nation arises only in resistance to foreign invasion. And just as in Iraq, Afghanistan's neighbors will not let pass the chance to prevent it from becoming a democracy.

America's definable enemies—the nations that sponsor Islamic terrorism—have been fortunate that we have sunk in the self-imposed quagmire of nation-building in Iraq and Afghanistan. By choosing to fight their proxies instead of them, we have not moved closer to victory but away from it. As we leave Iraq, the picture in our rearview mirror is dimly lit with fleeting images of purple-thumbed voters, victims of street bombings, and the smiling visage of Moqtada al-Sadr.

Our enemies have learned much about us in the decade since 9/11. It is not clear that we have learned much, if anything, about them. Or about ourselves.

Obama's War Tactics Are Subtle Yet Deadly

Luiza Ch. Savage

Luisa Ch. Savage covers American politics for the Canadian magazine Macleans.

President Barack Obama has moved American warfare tactics away from the "shock and awe" that former president George W. Bush favored, writes Savage in the following article. But this does not mean that Obama's tactics are any less deadly. Obama, Savage states, favors small, tactical strikes against specific targets rather than widespread battles. These attacks minimize US casualties and receive less attention. Obama has received much criticism for his tactics, which some label the Obama Doctrine. Defenders call Obama's approach "practical and realistic." It remains to be seen, Savage writes, whether Obama will be successful at diplomacy and providing developmental aid to the countries that have been altered due to US policies.

Barack Obama used U.S. air power to prevent a massacre and facilitate the overthrow of Moammar Gadhafi in Libya. He sent a team of Navy SEALs [an elite special operations force] to conduct a secret surgical strike in Pakistan that took out Osama bin Laden, America's public enemy number one [and the mastermind behind the 9/11 attacks]. He sent a Predator drone [unmanned plane] armed with Hellfire missiles to assassinate an American citizen in Yemen, Anwar al-Awlaki, whose extremist preaching was linked to several attempted terrorist attacks against the U.S. All three objectives were achieved without invasion, occupation, or the loss of American lives.

Luiza Ch. Savage, "Obama the Hawk: Sure, He's Pulling Troops Out of Iraq, but He's Found Lethal New Ways to Flex America's Military Muscle," *Maclean's Magazine*, vol. 124, no. 44, November 14, 2011, p. 44. Reproduced by permission.

A Shift in Tactics

The last decade was dominated by the [George W.] Bush administration's "shock and awe" display of U.S. military might, a swagger that descended into a "long war" of occupation and nation building in Afghanistan and Iraq that left thousands of Americans dead and wounded, and cost upward of a trillion dollars. But cold, calculating and nimble, Obama has turned a new page on the projection of American power. His emphasis on technology, intelligence, and leaning on allies is leaving a smaller and less costly U.S. military footprint on the globe, but one that is proving to be just as lethal to its adversaries.

In his first days as President, Obama ordered interrogation techniques cleaned up and the prison at Guantanamo Bay [Cuba] to be closed within a year. Congress objected, and Guantanamo has remained open, but the President has added zero detainees to the inmate population. Indeed, he's barely taken any prisoners—instead, he has presided over many more drone strikes against terrorist suspects than George W. Bush. He is not waterboarding [torturing] enemy prisoners who have been removed from the battle field; he is killing them where they stand. (The administration denies frequent accusations that it is killing militants when capturing them would have been feasible.)

Ending the Iraq War

Last week [October 21, 2011], Obama announced that all U.S. troops would leave Iraq by the end of the year. The White House presented the move as the fulfillment of a campaign promise to end the war, despite the fact that the administration had pressed the Iraqi government to allow the troops to stay beyond the Dec. 31 deadline that had been agreed to by Bush. When Iraq would not agree to immunity from prosecution for U.S. soldiers, Obama announced they were heading home. But Obama's cutting the number of U.S. troops deployed abroad should not be confused with an end to U.S. interventionism. In October, with the Libya mission still under way, Obama ordered 100 U.S. combat troops into central Africa to train and assist four African nations in the hunt for Joseph Kony, the murderous leader of the Lord's Resistance Army who has been indicted at The Hague for crimes against humanity.

The move once again had Obama's signature approach: a specific target, a small U.S. military force, and reliance on American technology and expertise to enhance the capabilities of foreign local and allied forces. "If the Bush administration was—at least in the first term—about using 'shock and awe' power and trying to bend the will of the world with our unparalleled military force, and if [Bush's secretary of state Colin] Powell doctrine was about employing maximum military force in a particular situation, then you could say the Obama administration's use of force is about being precise and principled," says Brian Katulis, a senior fellow in national security at the Center for American Progress, a Washington think tank. Obama's decision to give a defined end date for his troop ramp up in Afghanistan is evidence of his dislike of open-ended military commitments and nation building, Kamlis adds.

The Obama Doctrine

The approach is a new "Obama Doctrine" argues David Rothkopf, a scholar at the Carnegie Endowment for International Peace. "Obama & Co. embrace the arthroscopic [minimally invasive] alternative to the open-heart surgery favored by the Bush team;" he wrote in a *Foreign Policy* magazine essay. "The Obama Doctrine prioritizes the use of intelligence, unmanned aircraft, special forces, and the leverage of teaming with others to achieve very narrowly defined but critical goals."

The increasing overlap of intelligence and military functions was brought into focus when Obama appointed his CIA

[Central Intelligence Agency] chief, Leon Panetta, to take over the Pentagon as defence secretary, and moved a top general, David Petraeus, to head up the CIA. The swap underscored one of the biggest changes in the evolving U.S. security apparatus: the CIA is now as much about covert paramilitary operations, like drone strikes, as it is about intelligence analysis, while the military is increasingly focused on clandestine missions by elite squads of special forces. While the convergence of the intelligence and military approach began under the Bush administration, it has accelerated under Obama, who has deployed military special forces and CIA operatives—often working together—to many corners of the globe, from Yemen to Somalia to Afghanistan and Pakistan.

Obama has also deliberately set out to reestablish multilateral [multiple countries working together] military cooperation. In the early stages of the Bush administration, multilateralism was much maligned in the U.S.—Republicans denigrated it as "asking for a permission slip" from other countries. "I think Obama has turned multilateralism on its head—he's turned it into getting other countries to exercise their responsibilities," says Katulis. But the benefits come with a cost that evokes the old "permission slip" critique: the support of Arab countries for the Libya mission—and the lack of enthusiasm for doing something similar elsewhere—made the difference between the U.S. going after Gadhafi, but refraining from intervening in other nations where pro-democracy demonstrators were being killed.

After the death of Gadhafi, Obama made the case that multilateralism had been vindicated. "Without putting a single U.S. service member on the ground, we achieved our objectives, and our NATO [North Atlantic Treaty Organization] mission will soon come to an end" he declared. "We've demonstrated what collective action can achieve in the 21st century."

Obama's Critics

It remains to be seen how Obama's national security strategy will fare over the long haul. The approach has attracted many skeptics.

Some of the criticism is political. Republicans, hoping to portray Obama as weak on national security as they head into the 2012 election, portray his approach in Libya of primarily playing a supporting role for NATO allies—dubbed "leading from behind"—as weakening America's position in the world. "God did not create this country to be a nation of followers;" said Republican presidential hopeful Mitt Romney in a foreign policy speech on Oct. 7 [2011]. "America is not destined to be one of several equally balanced global powers. America must lead the world, or someone else will." Another Republican contender, Michele Bachmann, has also weighed in. "Obama's policy of leading from behind is an outrage," she said, Bachmann has repeatedly attacked Obama for committing U.S. air power to the Libya mission despite the lack of an "identifiable American vital interest"—and for pulling U.S. ground forces out of Iraq as scheduled.

Legal controversy surrounds another of Obama's tactics, the use of drones, and whether these targeted killings away from the "hot" battlefields of Afghanistan and Iraq amount to assassination. The new technology has quickly emerged as a central U.S. tactic, raising a myriad of new questions—from disputes about the number of civilian casualties that accompany the militant deaths, to questions about the process for adding names to a target list, and more forward-looking worries about what will happen as other countries inevitably acquire armed drones of their own. "We need a more political and philosophical debate over the use of drones," says Katulis. "I think it's amazing we are using this tool almost every day, in the absence of an overarching framework that discusses when might these campaigns be brought to an end. It could lead to this sort of war through robotics and technology."

There are also diplomatic concerns. Obama's own former director of national intelligence, Dennis Blair, has publicly criticized the administration for overemphasizing drones in its strategy in Pakistan. The attacks anger a Pakistani public concerned about reports of civilian deaths, and are failing to achieve the kind of co-operation necessary with Pakistan to truly root out militants, Blair argues. "Al Qaeda [militant Islamic organization responsible for the 9/11 attacks, among others] officials who are killed by drones will be replaced. The group's structure will survive and it will still be able to inspire, finance and train individuals and teams to kill Americans", argued Blair in a *New York Times* op-ed. "Our dogged persistence with the drone campaign is eroding our influence and damaging our ability to work with Pakistan to achieve other important security objectives like eliminating Taliban [Afghan resistance group removed in 2001 who want to regain power] sanctuaries, encouraging Indian-Pakistani dialogue, and making Pakistan's nuclear arsenal more secure."

Many Problems Remain

But for all the debate it has stoked, it is unclear whether Obama's approach adds up to a coherent military doctrine, as opposed to a set of *ad hoc* [situational] policies taken in response to individual circumstances.

"It would be a mistake to assume we have ushered in a new kind of warfare, as if letting others take the lead and using drones and cruise missiles will always be the answer," says Michael O'Hanlon, a senior fellow at the Brookings Institution, a Washington think tank. "If the administration believed there was an alternative to war, they would have pulled the 95,000 troops out of Afghanistan. You have to recognize that these new means of warfare have an important but limited applicability. Therefore the 'Obama Doctrine,' as such, applies to only a certain category of missions."

It would also be a mistake to credit Obama for having the insight that drones were a good idea. The Pentagon long ago realized the potential, but the technology was still in its infancy in the early Bush years. The Pentagon now has some 7,000 aerial drones, compared with fewer than 50 only a decade ago, and has asked Congress for nearly $5 billion for drones in 2012, according to the *New York Times*. "The fact that you see so many new technologies on the battlefield, giving operations a longer reach, is merely a function of the opportunities offered by new technologies" says retired U.S. Army Gen. Montgomery Meigs, a visiting professor of strategy and military operations at Georgetown University's School of Foreign Service. Meigs does not see a new paradigm in Obama's actions; he calls Obama's approach merely "pragmatic and realistic."

For all that, though, Obama's decision to wind down the Iraq war—even before the pullout this December—freed up many drones to prowl skies elsewhere in search of militants. To that extent, his tactics—and not just technological evolution—have made a difference.

Obama has shown he can wield American hard power. But the real test for the commander-in-chief comes next, and it may depend more on the soft-power spheres of diplomacy and development aid. With Gadhafi gone, who will run Libya? After U.S. forces leave Iraq, what kind of society will be left in their wake? And can Obama achieve the kind of co-operation necessary from Pakistan to root out the militants, rather than picking them off with drone strikes? "This administration faces the back side of the campaign," says Meigs. "This is a harder problem than the surge of emotion that leads us to go into Afghanistan to 'make sure al-Qaeda can't do that again.' The problem is more abstract and harder to control. In some ways this is bigger."

Middle East Revolutions May Not Lead to Democracy

Pauline H. Baker

Pauline H. Baker is a political scientist who is former president of the Fund for Peace, an educational and research organization based in Washington, DC. She has written extensively on American foreign policy.

In the following selection, Baker casts a critical eye on the so-called Arab Spring, a wave of revolutionary uprisings, protests, and demonstrations in the Middle East that began December 17, 2010, and led to the overthrow of rulers in Egypt, Tunisia, and and Libya. She argues that such revolutions do not necessarily presage a democratic society and that revolution is only the beginning: The aftermath of a governmental change is just as important. Baker advises that four basic concepts must be acknowledged for a country to effect substantial regime change: (1) the understanding that democratization is not a simple process; (2) that political volatility is common; (3) that all factions should be allowed representation in new governments; and (4) that elections, while important, are just a first step. Unless emerging democracies account for the above complications when planning for the future, Baker writes, they may slide back into dictatorship or further unrest.

Conventional thinking juxtaposes democracy and dictatorship as mutually exclusive systems. It is often assumed that when one system collapses, it is replaced by the other, as if this was the natural order of things. Some theorists, such as [American political scientist] Francis Fukuyama, argued that

Pauline H. Baker, "The Dilemma of Democratization in Fragile States," *UN Chronicle*, vol. 48, no. 4, December 2011, p. 34. Copyright © 2011 by United Nations Publishing. All rights reserved. Reproduced by permission.

liberal democracy had decisively defeated tyranny with the collapse of the Soviet Union, which marked the "end of history." Indeed, since then, while there have been setbacks in countries such as Ukraine and Zimbabwe, dictatorship has been in retreat.

Unfulfilled Promises

The most dramatic wave of change has been the Arab Spring [a wave of Middle East uprisings], in which strongmen in North Africa and the Middle East have been deposed since January 2011. In less dramatic fashion, several countries in sub-Saharan Africa have also moved incrementally toward democratic rule over the last decade. According to *The Economist*, since 1991, 30 parties or leaders in sub-Saharan Africa have been removed by voters. While outcomes have varied, and violence has sometimes followed, grass roots political action, not military rule or assassinations, is emerging as the primary method of removing unpopular leaders.

However, states often go through fleeting periods of democratic reform which may not fully materialize, or teeter in the balance for prolonged periods of time. Myanmar [formerly Burma] is an example of democracy crushed for half a century. The military has ruled since 1962, and the current junta [military group running the country] since 1988, when it violently suppressed a pro-democracy movement. In 2011, a civilian Government was installed, dominated by the same military or ex-military leaders. It initiated a series of positive steps, including giving more freedom to Daw Aung San Suu Kyi, the popular opposition leader who won the 1990 elections. The Government also loosened restrictions on the media and the Internet, suspended construction of a controversial hydroelectric dam supported by China, and released more than 200 political prisoners. While these steps are encouraging, Myanmar has far to go. It remains one of the most repressive and closed countries in the world, where the army

continues the repression of ethnic minorities, the main opposition political party was banned until November 2011 ...,
and hundreds more political prisoners languish in jail, though
the Government released some prisoners in October 2011.

Nigeria is an example of a country with democratic promise that remains unfulfilled. Credible elections were conducted
in 2011, the first since the return of civilian rule in 1999, and
it resulted in the historic installation of a president from a
minority ethnic group. Yet this singular event, which deservedly earned worldwide praise, did not fundamentally change
the political system. While there is a vibrant press, an increasingly active civil society and an enterprising population, the
country faces formidable problems, including ethnic, religious,
and economic friction; endemic corruption; severe economic
inequality; deepening violence; and a political culture dominated by competing cliques of ex-generals and business tycoons who act as behind-the-scenes power-brokers. Thus,
while Myanmar remains an authoritarian State with inklings
of political reform, Nigeria is an electoral democracy with undemocratic traits. In neither country is democratization assured.

Mixed Outcomes

In 1989, there was widespread hope for democratic transformation when the Berlin Wall [a barrier constructed by East
Germany in 1961 that cut West Berlin off from East Berlin
and East Germany and prevented East Germans from defecting to the West] came down. However, the death knell for authoritarianism had not rung in many of the capitals of the
successor republics that followed the collapse of the Soviet
Union, especially in Central Asia. In Russia, a popular leader
with a KGB [national security agency] background [namely,
Vladmir Putin] appealed to his people's desire for order and
national pride over the chaos of a criminal oligarchy [rule by

a small group] and the loss of superpower status. The result was "managed democracy," which cloaked authoritarian rule in democratic trappings.

Mixed outcomes are also possible in the Middle Eastern countries embroiled in the Arab Spring and in African States struggling with democratization. Most lack the historical experience, institutional foundations, and social consensus to undergo smooth transitions. There are no preordained outcomes. The leadership, timeframe, resources, and circumstances are different in each transition. Positive results have been seen, for example, in [the West African nation of] Liberia, despite two civil wars that killed an estimated 250,000 people. President Ellen Johnson Sirleaf, the first elected female African Head of State, who was awarded the Nobel Peace Prize in 2011, succeeded in preventing a recurrence of fighting, getting international debt relief, attracting economic aid, and keeping her country on track toward democracy since she was first elected in 2005. Despite that, Liberia remains a fragile State.

Elections are an essential part of democratization, but they can also be conflict-inducing if they are held too soon, are blatantly manipulated, lack transparency, or are marred by violence. Moreover, even if conducted efficiently, they may result in power shifts that not only marginalize powerful elites, but entire communities, creating sectarian or ethnic conflict. The Kenyan elections in 2007 did both.

In Nigeria, Northerners did not feel that the 2011 elections were free and fair, as most observers reported. The north—the poorest region in the country—is where most of the post-election violence which killed hundreds was concentrated, and where, perhaps not coincidentally, terrorist incidents attributed to Boko Haram, a radical Islamist movement, have escalated since the polling.

Populations may be loath to return to old authoritarian rulers, but they also do not want to see continued violence. Thus, after a full-blown conflict or revolutionary change, they often turn to new strongmen as saviours to impose order on chaos—often based on clan, ethnic, or religious identities. There is also a temptation to grasp for quick solutions, hold snap elections, push through slap-dash constitutional arrangements, use shotgun power-sharing agreements, or defer to transitional councils led by security forces—measures that undermine the foundation for democracy.

State-Building

In truth, the biggest danger facing fragile states in transition is not the rise of a new dictatorship, as is often assumed, or even the emergence of extremist factions, which usually represent a minority of the population. These outcomes are possible, but the larger threats are civil war, state collapse, mass atrocities, humanitarian emergencies, and a possible break-up of the country.

One way to avoid such scenarios is to institute an intermediate process of state-building, focusing not only on writing a new constitution, holding elections, and providing for basic freedoms, but also on building or restructuring core state institutions: the police, military, civil service, and judiciary, legislative and executive branches of Government. State-building cannot be bypassed by political accommodation. There still needs to be a solid state infrastructure for long-term stability, the provision of public services, adherence to the rule of law, and promotion of economic opportunity.

Thus far, [the North African nation] Tunisia has provided the best model of how it should be done. Within a year of driving its former authoritarian leader into exile, Tunisia became the first Arab Spring country to hold elections for a constituent assembly to write a new constitution and appoint an interim Government. The gradual and ordered political transition will allow time for the people to shape the structure of Government, and for new political formations to emerge, including political parties and civil society. Most of all, it af-

Released from home detention in 2011 after years of confinement by Myanmar's dictatorial government, activist Aung San Suu Kyi became the leader of the National League for Democracy party. With a civilian government in place, by-elections were held in April 2012, and she was elected by voters to represent Kawhmu Township in parliament. © Nyein Chan Naing/epa/Corbis.

fords the interim Government the chance to lay out a road-map for the future, including how to structure the transfer of power and set up state institutions. South Africa followed a similar path during its four-year-long transition to a post-apartheid society, from the time that anti-apartheid parties were legalized and political prisoners released in 1990, until the landmark election of Nelson Mandela in 1994. That interim period was crucial for laying the foundation for a peaceful and lasting democratic transition. It was remarkable that there was no external military intervention nor, contrary to widespread expectations, a race war, a collapse of the state, or a return to political violence.

Guidelines for External Parties

Democratization in fragile states is a complex process that cannot be rushed nor taken for granted. All parties should be cognizant of certain realities. First, there is no such thing as an instant democracy. No assumptions should be made about the capacity of fragile states to fulfil their democratic aspirations, nor should their capacity to do so be underestimated. What is important is that, whatever the capacity of the newly-formed state to transform itself, the process will not occur overnight.

This leads to the second reality—vacillation, even back-sliding, are not uncommon. Most states in democratic transition are embarking upon huge tasks—the rebuilding of the state, restoring national cohesion, and creating a representative government. As long as the general trend is in the right direction one can expect setbacks along the way. Volatility—not stability—is the natural order of things in the march to democracy.

Third, there must be political inclusion with all major factions allowed to present their views for open political discussion, debate, and political participation. However, a minority of spoilers can be destructive. Thus, in fragile states undergoing rapid change, groups or individuals that openly advocate violence, use hate speech, maintain their own militias, or engage in illegal practices should be restricted from running for public office and held accountable under the law so they do not ignite a new wave of retribution or revenge. If former warlords and power-brokers want to move from the battlefield to the ballot box, they should be allowed to do so, provided they give up their arms and refrain from keeping private armies in reserve in case they lose elections. Here the international community can be of vital assistance by providing technical support for the disarmament, demobilization [disbanding of troops], and reintegration of former combatants; supplying legal aid to institute the rule of law; offering financial assistance to get the economy going; and training professionals to run state institutions honestly and efficiently.

Fourth, the conditions must be right for holding elections—a secure and safe environment which allows for a proper nomination process, unrestricted media coverage, full and open campaigning by candidates, and citizen participation without intimidation. There must be electoral transparency, independent monitoring, and a well-trained election staff overseen by a commission of respected individuals, with sufficient authority and financial resources to meet the logistical challenges of nationwide voting, which often takes place over several days, in remote areas, and under extreme weather conditions. While it may sound contradictory, elections are not only an all-important pivotal milestone in a democratic transition, but merely the first step. The real tests will come in the second and third elections, and those that come after, when power is transferred peacefully from one party to another.

The Balancing Act

Beji Caid Essebsi, the 84-year-old transitional Prime Minister of Tunisia, faced a series of protests after the overthrow of the ousted dictator, Zine el-Abidine Ben Ali, with Tunisians demanding jobs, wages, and immediate retribution against the former rulers. It was not always clear that the transition would be a smooth one. Essebsi summarized the dilemma that he and other leaders across the Middle East and Africa are facing today: "Sometimes the proponents of freedom have demands that go beyond logic, and it is more difficult to protect freedom from the proponents of freedom themselves, than from the enemies," he said. "When someone is hungry asking for food, you only give him what he needs,' Essebsi noted, describing his step-by-step approach. 'You don't give him more, or else he might die".

The collapse of tyranny, Essebsi seems to be saying, is not the end of history: it is just the beginning. Democracy mismanaged, or descending too quickly, could kill nascent freedom, while democracy delayed, or descending too slowly, might lead to a new dictatorship or inspire further insurrection.

For Further Discussion

1. How do Hemingway's own experiences with war, specifically the Spanish Civil War, come into play in *For Whom the Bell Tolls*? See the selections by Moreira, Nakjavani, and the *Gale Contextual Encyclopedia of American Literature*.

2. According to Benson, what was Hemingway's own political stance during the Spanish Civil War, and how is it reflected in *For Whom the Bell Tolls*?

3. Why did Hemingway decide to show all sides of the war and not merely to write *For Whom the Bell Tolls* as a Loyalist? See selections by Hemingway, Benson, and Messent.

4. After consulting the selections by Moreira, Messent, and Nakjavani, discuss Hemingway's attitude toward warfare and how it is depicted in *For Whom the Bell Tolls*.

5. How does Robert Jordan's philosophy about war differ from that of earlier Hemingway heroes, and how is his attitude a reflection of Hemingway's own changing ideas? Refer to the selections by Hays and Donaldson.

6. Why is Pilar's massacre story of central importance to the novel, and how does its inclusion suggest Hemingway's own politics during the Spanish Civil War? See the selection by Josephs.

7. Consulting the article by Schwartz, discuss the similarities between America's wars in Afghanistan and Iraq and the Spanish Civil War. How, according to Schwartz, might lessons learned from the Spanish Civil War be applied today?

For Further Reading

Stephen Crane, *The Red Badge of Courage*, 1895.

Joseph Heller, *Catch-22*, 1961.

Ernest Hemingway, *The Complete Short Stories of Ernest Hemingway*, 1987.

Ernest Hemingway, *A Farewell to Arms*, 1929.

Ernest Hemingway, *The Fifth Column, and Four Stories of the Spanish Civil War*, 1969.

Ernest Hemingway, *The Sun Also Rises*, 1926.

Michael Herr, *Dispatches*, 1977.

Homer, *The Iliad*, c. 7th century B.C.

Norman Mailer, *The Naked and the Dead*, 1948.

André Malraux, *Man's Fate (La Condition humaine)*, 1933.

André Malraux, *Man's Hope (L'Espoire)*, 1937.

Tim O'Brien, *The Things They Carried*, 1990.

George Orwell, *Homage to Catalonia*, 1938.

Erich Maria Remarque, *All Quiet on the Western Front*, 1929.

Anthony Swofford, *Jarhead*, 2003.

Leo Tolstoy, *War and Peace*, 1863–1869.

Dalton Trumbo, *Johnny Got His Gun*, 1939.

Kurt Vonnegut, *Slaughterhouse-Five*, 1969.

Bibliography

Books

Carlos Baker   *Ernest Hemingway: Critiques of Four Major Novels.* New York: Scribner's, 1962.

Carlos Baker   *Hemingway: A Life Story.* New York: Scribner's, 1961.

Sheridan Baker   *Ernest Hemingway: An Introduction and Interpretation.* New York: Holt, Rinehart & Winston, 1967.

Antony Beevor   *The Battle for Spain: The Spanish Civil War, 1936–1939.* New York: Penguin, 2006.

Frederick R. Benson   *Writers in Arms: The Literary Impact of the Spanish Civil War.* New York: New York University Press, 1967.

Peter L. Bergen   *The Longest War: The Enduring Conflict Between America and al-Qaeda.* New York: Free Press, 2011.

Lawrence R. Broer   *Vonnegut and Hemingway: Writers at War.* Columbia: University of South Carolina Press, 2011.

Lawrence R. Broer and Gloria Holland   *Hemingway and Women: Female Critics and the Female Voice.* Tuscaloosa: University of Alabama Press, 2002.

Frieda S. Brown
Rewriting the Good Fight: Critical Essays on the Literature of the Spanish Civil War. East Lansing: Michigan State University Press, 1989.

Anthony Burgess
Ernest Hemingway and His World. New York: Scribner's, 1978.

Calvin F. Exoo
The Pen and the Sword: Press, War, and Terror in the 21st Century. Thousand Oaks, CA: Sage, 2010.

Helen Graham
The Spanish Civil War: A Very Short Introduction. Oxford: Oxford University Press, 2005.

Leo Gurko
Ernest Hemingway and the Pursuit of Heroism. New York: Crowell, 1968.

Ernest Hemingway and Sean A. Hemingway
Hemingway on War. New York: Scribner's, 2003.

Lee Bennett Hopkins and Stephen Alcorn
America at War. New York: Margaret K. McElderry Books, 2008.

Richard B. Hovey
Hemingway: The Inward Terrain. Seattle: University of Washington Press, 1968.

Gabriel Jackson
A Concise History of the Spanish Civil War. New York: John Day, 1974.

Seth G. Jones
In the Graveyard of Empires: America's War in Afghanistan. New York: Norton, 2009.

Sebastian Junger   *War.* New York: Twelve, 2010.

A.R. Lee   *Ernest Hemingway, New Critical
                    Essays.* London: Vision, 1983.

Kenneth S. Lynn   *Hemingway.* New York: Simon and
                    Schuster, 1987.

John K.M.   *Ernest Hemingway: The Man and His
McCaffery   Work.* New York: Cooper Square,
                    1969.

James R. Mellow   *Hemingway: A Life Without
                    Consequences.* Boston: Houghton
                    Mifflin, 1992.

Jeffrey Meyers   *Hemingway: A Biography.* New York:
                    Harper & Row, 1985.

Peter Monteath   *Writing the Good Fight: Political
                    Commitment in the International
                    Literature of the Spanish Civil War.*
                    Westport, CT: Greenwood, 1994.

Janet Pérez and   *The Spanish Civil War in Literature.*
Wendell M.   Lubbock: Texas Tech University Press,
Aycock   1990.

Michael Reynolds   *Hemingway: The 1930s.* New York:
                    Norton, 1997.

Earl Rovit   *Ernest Hemingway.* New York:
                    Twayne, 1963.

Francisco J.   *The Spanish Civil War: Origins,
Romero Salvadó   Course, and Outcomes.* Hampshire,
                    UK: Palgrave Macmillan, 2005.

Patrick W. Shaw | *The Modern American Novel of Violence.* Troy, NY: Whitston, 2000.

Alvin Toffler and Heidi Toffler | *War and Anti-war: Survival at the Dawn of the 21st Century.* Boston: Little, Brown, 1993.

Alex Vernon | *Hemingway's Second War: Bearing Witness to the Spanish Civil War.* Iowa City: University of Iowa Press, 2011.

Linda Wagner-Martin | *Ernest Hemingway: Eight Decades of Criticism.* East Lansing: Michigan State University Press, 2009.

Periodicals and Internet Sources

Gerry Brenner | "Epic Machinery in Hemingway's *For Whom the Bell Tolls*," *Modern Fiction Studies*, vol. 16, no. 4, 1970.

Ramon Buckley | "Revolution in Ronda: The Facts in Hemingway's *For Whom the Bell Tolls*," *Hemingway Review*, Fall 1997.

Robert Gajdusek | "Pilar's Tale: The Myth and the Message," *Hemingway Review*, Fall 1990.

Stacey Guill | "Pilar and Maria: Hemingway's Feminist Homage to the 'New Woman of Spain' in *For Whom the Bell Tolls*," *Hemingway Review*, Winter 2011.

Allen Guttmann   "Mechanized Doom: Ernest Hemingway and the Spanish Civil War," *Massachusetts Review*, vol. 1, no. 3, 1960.

Marc Hewson   "A Matter of Love or Death: Hemingway's Developing Psychosexuality in *For Whom the Bell Tolls*," *Studies in the Novel*, vol. 36, no. 2, 2004.

Michael Hirsh   "The 10-Year Tragedy," *National Journal*, October 6, 2011.

Alfred Kazin   "The Wound That Will Not Heal: Writers and the Spanish Civil War," *New Republic*, August 25, 1986.

Frank Ledwidge   "Permanent War Is a Disaster for Us All," *New Statesman*, March 19, 2012.

Alex Link   "Rabbit at the Riverside: Names and Impossible Crossings in Hemingway's *For Whom the Bell Tolls*," *Hemingway Review*, Fall 2009.

Stephen Marche   "We Are All Heroes," *Esquire*, March 2012.

Jeffrey Meyers   "Hemingway's Humor," *Michigan Quarterly Review*, Spring 2004.

Jonathan Rauch   "Partisan Retreat: Our Inevitable Withdrawal from Iraq Could Poison American Politics for a Generation," *Atlantic Monthly*, January–February 2008.

Sarah R. Shaber — "Hemingway's Literary Journalism: The Spanish Civil War Dispatches," *Journalism Quarterly*, vol. 57, no. 3, 1980.

David Sanders — "Ernest Hemingway's Spanish Civil War Experience," *American Quarterly*, Summer 1960.

Walter J. Slatoff — "The 'Great Sin' in *For Whom the Bell Tolls*," *Journal of Narrative Technique*, Spring 1977.

Michael K. Solow — "A Clash of Certainties, Old and New: *For Whom the Bell Tolls* and the Inner War of Ernest Hemingway," *Hemingway Review*. Fall 2010.

Susan Stamberg — "Robert Jordan, Hemingway's Bipartisan Hero," NPR Books. www.npr.org.

Ben Stoltzfus — "Hemingway, Malraux and Spain: *For Whom the Bell Tolls* and *L'espoir*," *Comparative Literature Studies*, 1999.

Creath S. Thorne — "The Shape of Equivocation in Ernest Hemingway's *For Whom the Bell Tolls*," *American Literature*, vol. 51, no. 4, 1980.

Lisa A. Twomey — "Taboo or Tolerable? Hemingway's *For Whom the Bell Tolls* in Postwar Spain," *Hemingway Review*, Winter 2011.

Michael Ware — "They Say It's Over—," *Newsweek*, January 2, 2012.

Robert F. Worth   "The Desert War," *New York Times Magazine*, July 11, 2010.

Index

A

Across the River and into the Trees (Hemingway), 14, 31, 43
Afghanistan War, 123–127, 143, 152
Africa, 29, 32
Alawi, Ayad, 147
Alfonso XIII, 10
Alienation, 67–68
Anderson, Sherwood, 25
André Marty (*For Whom the Bell Tolls*), 12, 14, 71, 83–84
Andrés (*For Whom the Bell Tolls*), 12, 71, 83–84, 88, 89, 91
Arab Spring, 157–165
Arnold, Matthew, 115
Aung San Suu Kyi, *162*

B

Babbin, Jed, 140–149
Bachmann, Michele, 154
Baker, Carlos, 58, 61, 110–115
Baker, Pauline H., 157–165
Batista, Fulgencio, 32
Beach, Sylvia, 25
Beevor, Antony, 15
Benson, Frederick R., 57–61
Berlin Wall, 159
Big Two-Hearted River (Hemingway), 26
Bin Laden, Osama, 124, 142, 143, 145, 150
Blair, Dennis, 155
Blair, Tony, 141
Bloom, Harold, 15–16

Boko Haram, 160
Boni & Liveright, 27
Brown, Tina, 131
Bruccoli, Matthew J., 9, 14–15
Bullfighting, 29, 32
Burma, 158–159
Bush, George W., 141–144, 151
Bush administration, 128–130, 132–133, 141

C

Camus, Albert, 139
Carlism, 138
Castro, Fidel, 32
Casualties, 11, 15, 40, 88
Central Intelligence Agency (CIA), 152–153
Cézanne, Paul, 26
Che Ti Dice La Patria (Hemingway), 59
Cheney, Richard, 141
China, 41–42
Clark, Greg, 34–35
A Clean, Well-Lighted Place (Hemingway), 29
Cohen, Ariel, 135
Collier's, 30, 39, 43, 44
Communism/communists, 15, 54, 59, 80
Cooper, Anderson, 28–29
Courage, 94
Couric, Katie, 130
Cowles, Virginia, 40
Crook Factory, 30
Cuba, 30–31, 32

D

D-Day, 31, 43–44
Death
    facing, 97, 102
    in *For Whom the Bell Tolls*, 95,
        96–102
    Hemingway's attitude toward,
        45
    by suicide, 98
Death in the Afternoon
    (Hemingway), 29
Democratic transitions, 157–166
Donaldson, Scott, 96–102
Dos Passos, John, 40
Drone warfare, 150, 154–155, 156

E

The Economist, 123–127
Elections, 160, 164
Electroshock therapy, 33
Eliot, T.S., 26, 112
Engels, Friedrich, 54
Epic literature, 110–115
Espionage, 41
Esquire, 29
Essebsi, Beji Caid, 164–165

F

Failure, 14
A Farewell to Arms (Hemingway)
    commitment to cause in, 93
    hero of, 37
    heroism in, 75–77
    inspiration for, 38
    narrative perspective in, 70
    preface to, 53
    sense of futility in, 12–13
    success of, 28

war in, 9
    writing of, 27
Fascists/fascism, 10, 12, 47–50, 54,
    59, 80, 86–87
Female characters, 91–93, 116–121
Fenichel, Otto, 116
Fenimore, Edward, 114
The Fifth Column (Hemingway),
    41
Fitzgerald, F. Scott, 27
For Whom the Bell Tolls
    (Hemingway)
    background of, 64
    characters in, 91–93
    commitment to cause in,
        86–95
    death and dying in, 95, 96–
        102
    dialogue in, 89–90
    as epic, 110–115
    even handedness of, 14–15
    failure as theme of, 14
    female characters in, 91–93,
        116–121
    film adaptation of, *92, 106,
        119*
    guerrilla fighters in, 82–83, 87
    heroism in, 86–95
    holding of the bridge in, 110–
        112
    interior discourse in, 72–74
    lack of propaganda in, 83–85
    language in, 89–91, 113–115
    massacre story in, 103–109,
        119
    narrative perspective in, 9,
        70–74
    plot of, 87
    prose techniques in, 89–91
    protagonist of, 64–65, 69–74,
        87, 96
    realism in, 89–91, 109

reception of, 29–30, 86
theme of, 12
title of, 68
violence depicted in, 13, 14,
88, 90–91, 94–95, 103–109,
117–118
war depicted in, 41, 69–95
writing of, 29
Franco, Francisco, 9, 10, 12, 39,
135, 136, *137*
Fraser, Ronald, 80
Frederic Henry (*A Farewell to
Arms*), 36–37, 70–72, 75–77, 99
Fukuyama, Francis, 157–158

G

Gadhafi, Moammar, 150
Gajdusek, Robert E., 105–107
*Gale Contextual Encyclopedia of
American Literature*, 23–33
The Garden of Eden (Hemingway),
32
Gellhorn, Martha, 29–30, 39–41,
43, 44, 79
Germany, 10, 50, 61, 80, 139, 159
Greco-Turkish War, 35, 38–39
Green Hills of Africa
(Hemingway), 29
Guantanamo Bay, 151
Guernica (Picasso), 88, 109
Guerrilla fighters, 80–83, 87

H

Hays, Peter L., 86–95
Heath, Edward, 135
Hemingway, Ernest
attitude of, toward death, 45
childhood of, 24
depictions of war by, 69–95

in Europe, 25–27, 31, 43–44
injuries sustained by, 36–37
as journalist, 24–25
later years of, 31–33
life of, 23–33, 63–64
marriages of, 25, 27, 30, 31,
40, 45, 46
photos of, *28, 42, 67, 82*
politics of, 14–15, 57–61
post-traumatic stress experienced by, 46
on Spanish Civil War, 14–15
suicide of, 33
travels of, 9, 26, 29, 32
views of, on war, 9, 28, 52–56,
65
on war correspondents, 47–51
war experiences of, 9, 25, 29–
31, 34–46, 63–64
works of, 26–32
writing goal of, 9–10
Hemingway, Gregory, 29
Hemingway, Hadley, 25, 27
Hemingway, John, 26
Hemingway, Pauline, 27, 29, 39, 40
Hemingway code, 37
Herbst, Josephine, 9
Heroes, 66–70, 77–78, 116–117
Heroism, 75–77, 86–95
Hitler, Adolf, 9, 12
Homage to Catalonia (Orwell), 108
Homer, 113, 115
Hussein, Saddam, 142–145, 148

I

Iftikhar, Shabnum, 63–68
Iliad (Homer), 113
In Our Time (Hemingway), 27, 72
Interior discourse, 72–74, 90
Iran, 147

Iraq War
    controversy over, 141–142
    cost of, 142
    end of, 140–141, 151–152
    failure of, 140–149
    media-fueled run-up to, 128–133
    Spanish Civil War and, 134–139
    violence in, 145–147
Islamofacism, 139
Italy, 10, 50, 61, 80
Ivens, Joris, 41, 49

J

Jaspers, Karl, 56
Josephs, Allen, 9–10, 103–109
Joyce, James, 26
Jung, Carl, 105

K

Kansas City Star, 24–25
Kashkin (*For Whom the Bell Tolls*), 98–99
Kashkin, Ivan, 70–71
Kastely, James L., 72
Katulis, Brian, 152, 153, 154
Kenya, 160
Kipling, Rudyard, 123
Kony, Joseph, 152
Korean War, 46
Kurds, 137, 143, 147, 148

L

La Pasionaria, 80
Lanhara, Charles, 44
Lawrence, T.E., 82–83
Leclerc, Philippe, 43

Leftist causes, 14–15
Lenin, Vladimir, 59
Lewis, Wyndham, 60
Liberia, 160
Libya, 150, 153, 154
Lieberman, Joseph, 134–135, 139
Literary themes, 59–60
Lorca, Federico Garcia, 138
Lost Generation, 28, 64, 65–66
Loyalists, 10, 15, 80, 87

M

MacShane, Denis, 135
Al-Maliki, Nouri, 147, 148
Malraux, André, 12
Maria (*For Whom the Bell Tolls*), 87, 88, 91–93, 98, 116–121
Marty, André, 14
Marx, Karl, 54
Massacre passage, 103–109, 119
Matisse, Henri, 26
McCain, John, 16
McClellan, Scott, 128–130, 133
Meachem, John, 16
Media, Iraq war and, 128–133
Meigs, Montgomery, 156
Messent, Peter, 69–78
Meyers, Jeffrey, 15, 41, 79–85
Middle East revolutions, 157–165
Miller, Judith, 131–132
Mississippi to Madrid (Yates), 11–12
Moreira, Peter, 34–46
Morgenthau, Henry, Jr., 41
A Moveable Feast (Hemingway), 32
Multilateralism, 153
Mussolini, Benito, 9, 12, 59

Myanmar, 158–159
Myers, Richard, 144

N

Nakjavani, Erik, 52–56
Napoleon, 79–80, 81
Narrative techniques, 70–74,
  90–91
Nasrallah, Hassan, 139
Nationalists, 87
Nation-building, 149, 152, 161,
  163
Nazis, 54, 139
Neruda, Pablo, 12
Nietzsche, Friedrich, 105
Nigeria, 159, 160
Nin, Andreu, 138
Nobel Prize in Literature, 32
Noble causes, futility of, 12–13
Nolan, Charles J., Jr., 116–121
North American Newspaper Alli-
  ance (NANA), 39
North Atlantic Treaty Organiza-
  tion (NATO), 124, 125, 153
Notes on the Next War
  (Hemingway), 54
Nothingness, 66–68

O

Obama, Barack, 16, 124, 140, 142,
  150–156
Obama Doctrine, 152–153, 155–
  156
Office of Strategic Services (OSS),
  42
O'Hanlon, Michael, 155
The Old Man and the Sea
  (Hemingway), 31–32

The Old Man at the Bridge
  (Hemingway), 11
Omar, Mullah, 143
Omniscient narration, 71–72
Orwell, George, 12, 29, 108

P

Pablo (*For Whom the Bell Tolls*),
  76–77, 83, 84, 87, 88, 91, 107
Paco Berrendo (*For Whom the Bell
  Tolls*), 95
Pakistan, 125–126, 155
Panetta, Leon, 153
Paris, France, 25–26, 31, 43
Patriotism run amok, 130–132
Patton, George, 31
Pelkey, Red, 44, 45
Peninsular War, 79–82, 84
Petraeus, David, 141, 146–147,
  148, 153
Pfeiffer, Pauline. *See* Hemingway,
  Pauline
Picasso, Pablo, 26, 88, 109
Pilar (*For Whom the Bell Tolls*)
  commitment to cause by,
    93–94
  in film adaptation, *106*
  massacre story told by, 88,
    90–91, 103–109, 119
  prophecy by, 83, 97
  strength of, 87, 91–93
Pipes, Daniel, 135
PM, 30, 41
Points of view, 71–72
Political causes, 14–15, 57–61, 67,
  86–95
Post-traumatic stress disorder
  (PTSD), 116, 120–121
Postwar trauma, 46

Pound, Ezra, 25–26
Powell, Colin, 132, 144, 152
Propaganda, 14, 15, 58–59, 79–85, 108
Prose techniques, 89–91, 113–115
Putin, Vladmir, 159–160

Q

Al-Qaeda, 125, 133, 144, 145, 146–147, 155

R

Rafael (*For Whom the Bell Tolls*), 90
Rather, Dan, 131
Realism, 89–91, 109
Red Cross ambulance corps, 36–37
Revolutionary uprisings, in Middle East, 157–165
Reynolds, Michael, 45, 46
Richardson, Hadley. *See* Hemingway, Hadley
Robert Jordan (*For Whom the Bell Tolls*)
  actions of, 84, 94–95, 111–112
  death of, 97, 102
  family history of, 99–102
  heroic qualities of, 69–70, 77–78, 94
  interior discourse by, 72–74, 90
  mission of, 12–14
  model for, 82–83
  as protagonist of novel, 64–65, 69–74, 87, 96
  self-division in, 74–75
  on war, 9
Romney, Mitt, 154

Rothkopf, David, 152
Rothschild, Matthew, 128–133
Rumsfeld, Donald, 133, 141, 144
Russia, 80–82, 159–160
  See also Soviet Union
Russian Revolution, 54

S

Al-Sadr, Moktada, 138, 147
Savage, Luiza Ch., 150–156
Schwartz, Stephen, 134–139
Second Sino-Japanese War, 35, 41–42
Second Spanish Republic, 10, 61
Self-division, 74–75
September 11, 2001, 124–125, 142
Sirleaf, Ellen Johnson, 160
Smith, Ronald, 116
Soldiers Home (Hemingway), 35
Solow, Michael K., 13
El Sordo (*For Whom the Bell Tolls*), 13, 15, 83–84, 91, 93, 97
South Africa, 163
Soviet Union, 10–11, 136, 158
  See also Russia
Spain, 9, 26, 136–138
Spanish Civil War, 9
  blame for loss in, 15
  brutality of, 88–89
  casualties in, 11, 15, 40, 88
  depicted in *For Whom the Bell Tolls*, 69–95
  events of, 10–12, 29, 40–41, 54
  Hemingway during, 29–30, 35, 39–41, 64
  Hemingway on, 14–15, 48–51
  Iraq War and, 134–139
  as noble cause, 13
  participants in, 10–12, 39, 64, 80

Peninsular War and, 79–82
politics of, 57–58, 60–61
The Spanish Earth (film), 41, 49
Stalin, Joseph, 59, 138
State-building, 161, 163
Stein, Gertrude, 25, 26
Stoneback, H.R., 105, 107–108
Sub-Saharan Africa, 158
Suicide, 33, 98
The Sun Also Rises (Hemingway),
9, 27, 28, 37, 70, 93
Sun Tzu, 55
Syria, 148

T

Taliban, 123, 124, 125, 127, 143
Tenet, George, 141, 144
Terrorists, 143–145, 146–147
Three Stories & Ten Poems
(Hemingway), 26
To Have and Have Not
(Hemingway), 29
Tolstoy, Leo, 9, 10, 15–16
Transatlantic Review, 26–27
Trotsky, Leon, 59
True at First Light (Hemingway),
32
Tunisia, 161, 164–165

U

United States, 11
U.S. war tactics, 150–156

V

Von Kurowsky, Agnes, 37–38

W

Wahhabism, 138
Walton, Bill, 45
War
atrocities of, 117–118
casualties in, 11, 15, 40
depiction of, by Hemingway,
69–78, 79–85
futility of, 67–68
guerrilla, 80–82
Hemingway's views on, 9, 28,
52–56, 65
propaganda, 14, 15, 58–59,
79–85, 108
self-division about, 74–75
U.S. tactics, 150–156
See also specific wars
War and Peace (Tolstoy), 9, 10, 15
War correspondents, 47–51
War epic, 110–115
Welsh, Mary, 31, 43, 44, 46
Wings over Africa (Hemingway),
55
Women. *See* Female characters
World War I, 25, 28, 35–38, 83
World War II, 30–31, 43–45
Wound theory, 37
Wyatt, David, 72

Y

Yates, James, 11–12
Yellin, Jessica, 129, 130
Young, Philip, 37, 60, 116

Z

Al Zarqawi, Abu Musab, 138, 144,
145